MAKING THE *ZEROS* COUNT

Making the Zeros Count: A Field Guide for Decamillionaires, Centimillionaires and Billionaires by Adam Katz

Library of Congress Number: 2025916488

ISBN: 978-1-959009-24-5 (eBook)
ISBN: 978-1-959009-25-2 (Paperback)

Published in the United States by Parallel Lines, Westfield, N.J.

This book is an independent publication by the author and is not sponsored, endorsed, or affiliated with Corient Holdings LLC or its affiliates ("Corient"). The views, opinions and advice expressed herein are solely those of the author and do not represent the views, policies of Corient. This publication is intended for educational and informational purposes only and is not considered Corient marketing, advertisement, solicitation, or promotional material for Corient's services. The information contained herein is for general informational purposes only and should not be considered financial, legal tax or investment advice. Readers should consult with qualified professionals regarding their specific circumstances before making any financial decisions.

All client examples, case studies and scenarios referenced in this book have been anonymized to protect client confidentiality. Any identifying information including personal characteristics have been changed or fictionalized. Any resemblance to actual persons or specific client situation is coincidental.

Advance Praise for Making the Zeros Count

"Adam has one of the sharpest minds in wealth advisory, but what truly sets him apart is how deeply he understands the psychology of the wealth creator. His blend of technical expertise and genuine empathy is very uncommon. Having known and worked with him for more than a decade, I can say that this book reflects the wisdom and guidance that have served me incredibly well. I hope it will do the same for you and your family."

– Johnny Ayers, Co-Founder & CEO of Socure

"I remember sitting with Adam at lunch jotting down my 'wish list' on an actual napkin. His framing within this book of how to think about money and the 'marginal utility' of additional dollars has been extremely empowering."

– Lauren Bosworth, Founder of LoveWellness

"The first time I met Adam, we spent almost three hours together. Even back then, he was always enumerating ideas within some framework. Adam really 'walks the walk and talks the talk' of concepts within this book."

– Jeff Braverman, Founder of Nuts.com

"While I was not seeking any help on investing my money, unbeknownst to me, I was seeking help on how to think about the purpose and role of money in my life. Adam's mindset and constructs helped me and will help anyone reading this book!"

– Eli Broverman, Co-Founder of Betterment

"In many ways, Adam and I have been on a parallel journey for the last 10+ years. From the first time we met, it was immediately obvious that he took a very differentiated approach to a typically indiscernible profession. He epitomizes the long game. As a person who's been betting on entrepreneurs for decades, if I could have invested in the equity of Adam Katz back then, I would have. Read this book and you'll understand why."

– Mark Peter Davis, Founder of Interplay

"I've loved investing since I was a kid. It was a topic at the dinner table. I never thought I needed an advisor until I met Adam. His frameworks within this book around money and the role it can play have been life-changing for me!"

– Morgan DeBaun, Founder of Blavity

"Adam's perspective has stayed with my wife and me long after we finished the book. His idea of 'random acts of kindness' reshaped the way we think about money—shifting us from a scarcity mindset to one of abundance. That reminder that a little extra generosity can change someone's day has, in many ways, impacted us even more than the people on the receiving end. It clarified what money is for and how small, intentional gestures can create real everyday impact. It's the kind of insight every entrepreneur navigating an exit should hear."

– Stephen Ellsworth, Co-Founder of Poppi

"I met Adam over a decade ago at a C-level peer group event. I really liked his energy and passion for the topics he was covering. As you pick up this book, you'll quickly understand why. He's been an extremely helpful guide for me on so many topics covered within this book, especially his emphasis on your 'life pie' and how you think about time not only in the present, but also the future. His ideas on these topics will help shape how you think about what's next—time with family and friends and vacations."

– Yony Feng, Co-Founder of Peloton; Co-Founder of Ernesta

"I've known Katz since Kindergarten and was not surprised when he set out to write a book, fulfilling his high school yearbook superlative of 'Class Writer.' He has always been smart, practical, warm, and looked at the world in a unique way. When I found myself in a dark place—adulthood with no financial savvy—I looked to him for guidance. I'm excited for people to have a chance to filter their financial life through his singular lens."

– Jen Flanz, Executive Producer, The Daily Show

"Adam's encouragement of my intentional memory-making with my family has been unwavering, along with his personal support and pursuit of impactful charitable endeavors closely aligned with my own. He truly lives what he teaches in this book, which makes him a uniquely credible voice."

– Noah Glass, Founder of OLO

"I am proud to have built a category-defining brand not only in quality, but also purpose. The types of conversations I've had with Adam over the past decade have helped shape many of my personal mindsets about money and meaning. Similar to my company's mission, my own relationship to money has helped me further many charitable endeavors. After all these years, I'm so glad he's sharing these ideas in his book, and I'm hopeful it will unlock a generosity and giving mindset for anyone reading it. The wealth management industry should be paying attention to this book!"

– Dave Heath, Co-Founder & Chairman of Bombas

"Adam Katz has a wise view of how to manage, invest, and spend money. Like in life, within this book he teaches how to build a relationship with money so that it can be a great tool to unlock the best potential for oneself and family. Having advised many successful individuals and worked closely with them, he has gained an incredible viewpoint on what constitutes sound wealth, how to build it, and how to manage it. I admire his effort to democratize the family office's secrets by publishing this book."

– Saeju Jeong, Co-Founder & Chairman of NOOM

"Adam's lens into the wealth creator is his superpower. While there are many books out there on how to think about life and money and how they all interact, his ideas explained in this book offer a different take on all of it. Much of what's in here will speak to his audience in a language they've never heard or read before."

– Jerry Lin, Co-Founder of Helix Sleep

"Adam Katz brings a thoughtful, client-first perspective to the financial lives of the wealthy. His focus on clarity, integrity, and truly understanding families shines through in his work. This book reflects the kind of forward-thinking approach our industry needs."

– Steve Lockshin, Founder of Vanilla, Convergent, Lydian, and AdvicePeriod; Author

"Adam has a unique ability to play the role of co-pilot for wealth creators across their entire journey, pre- to post-exit. He has an uncanny ability to get inside the heads of creators, find their whys, and provide practical guidance through approachable frameworks that evolve with you. This book will deeply resonate for those looking to invest time and money with intentionality."

– Joel Montaniel, Co-Founder & CEO of SevenRooms

"I call Adam my co-pilot. Sure, I could fly my own financial plane, but I prefer a pro like him at my side. In knowing Adam over the last decade, I've benefited from the ideas he's developed while working through moments of change alongside countless entrepreneurs and on his own founder's journey. If you want to hear from the rare advisor who knows the value of a life isn't measured in dollars, read this book."

– Scott Norton, Co-Founder of Sir Kensington's

"Talk about glass half full—this guy's cup is overflowing. I've known Adam for almost 15 years, and every time we get together, I'm genuinely excited to hear his new takes on so many aspects of life, and most importantly, living with focus and intentionality. Our conversations through the years have made a lasting impact on me."

– Gabe Plotkin, Co-Chairman & Owner of the Charlotte Hornets

"Adam has been an essential thought partner to me and my family for the interwoven journey through entrepreneurship and personal life. Since our first conversations over a decade ago, he's been an unwavering advocate of my most personal missions and goals for family, friends, and business. I love that he wrote a book after all this time and believe you'll enjoy his ideas as much as I do."

– Ryan Williams, Co-Founder of Cadre

MAKING THE *ZEROS* COUNT

A Field Guide for Decamillionaires, Centimillionaires and Billionaires

Adam Katz

Contents

Acknowledgments

I found it daunting to write this part of the book. I actually almost hit "print" without this section. That's not because I don't have a ton of folks to thank, but I suppose that I subconsciously fear that I'm going to 100% miss someone who should have been named. So, in a cowardly act, I will now ask for forgiveness for anyone who was surprised they weren't mentioned. It was likely an oversight! As you'll see, I actually cheated and don't name anyone, but you'll know who you are.

If I think of this as a bullseye, with concentric circles as well as some Venn diagramming, I'll attempt to layer my thanks in that construct.

Mom and Dad. You missed it all. Well, not all of it, but so many of the best parts for me and the family. And that will forever make me sad, particularly in moments like the publication of this book, when I need my parents' unwavering support and affirmation the most. I appreciate all the love and support for so many of the weird things people will read about in this book. You are the OG part of my origin story.

To my green-card-seeking wife, who will forever refer to me as her Club Med boy toy, I often say I can't imagine what it must be like to be married to me 😊. You're the best co-pilot I could have asked for.

To our secular holiday birthday children, in many ways you both inspired and fueled me to do so much of what is in this book, and

I'm hoping it's a meaningful part of both of your lives going forward. You have me on demand, but I also expect you both to read it when the time is right. And then use it as a reference guide throughout life.

To the rest of the 14 Sterling Place fam, there's a lot in here that will seem familiar, but perhaps like watching the behind-the-scenes clips from a movie you've seen 100x, but maybe never quite from the same angle. To the Montreal mishpacha and our family's Canadian "roots."

To my friends from summers at 01069, jingle jingle and make those arches. Supersized Fries. Supersized Diet Coke. To my friends who loved a cheeseburger at the diner when we still could digest them at midnight, and the one who always ordered a salad. To the Waltham crew, including the "true two colors gold and blue" brothers, to the one who grabbed my hand with the five-finger handshake and who now looks down from above, and to the fellow ice-cream scoopers…those were formative years.

To Building 20 and all that came with it back then, you guys shaped a lot of what's in here. Especially Mr. 173 outlook folders, Mr. Park Bench and Mr. UFC. To my mother Merrill brethren and, in particular, one of the main stars of the 1997 PCDP brochure.

To my KORE "krew," what a ride we have had. Some bumps, twists and turns, but any rollercoaster is full of all of that. And to my present partners. I didn't expect to make so many new friends on the back half and couldn't be having more fun. Look at me with a sports analogy to close it out. To the JCC crew and the AT2 and our gazillion talks about life, living and, well, this book. Snow Angels. To my mental trainer and our "real talks."

To my "book team," as I affectionately refer to you guys. Putting up with a first-time writer and guiding me through the unknown — I quite literally couldn't have created this without you. And last, but certainly the most, all the founders and entrepreneurs I have met along the way. This book quite literally couldn't exist without you. A sincere thank you.

PREAMBLE

THE WHY BEHIND MAKING THE ZEROS COUNT

This book is for people with insane, otherworldly financial wealth, at least by any normal human standards. I'm talking tens of millions of dollars to hundreds of millions, or even billions. Proverbial "f-you" money. It's largely for people who obtained it quickly in a "step function" wealth creation event, in which their ATM account-balance readout got elongated by two or three extra 0s—essentially overnight.

Most of the time, they sold a business or had a liquidity event of some sort, often with way more actuarial life ahead of them than behind them.

These are people who can do ANYTHING they want. But they often have no idea WHAT to do.

They arrived at exactly where they wanted to be, or so they thought, but not everything feels the way they expected. Having all the money you could ever spend is often oddly and surprisingly isolating. It's lonely. It's usually unexpectedly rife with judgment, expectations and envy.

Obviously, no one really feels bad for you. And no one really "gets it." You thought you reached the destination. The map looked intact. Your compass used to work. But now it sorta just spins as it did on the island in *Lost*.

You may be among the suddenly very wealthy or heading that way. This book will provide many frameworks to help. Think of it as the source code for WHAT to do next.

Meet your co-pilot

Now, who am I, and why am I even worth listening to? Well, first off, my day job is as a wealth advisor (although, to the chagrin of my wife, Dana, I often describe myself as a quasi-therapist or coach), with a *very* specific focus on first-generation wealth creators going through one of these "extra zeros" events. This daily vantage point gives me unique access to a lab to test all these ideas out. And iterate a lot until I know they work. But since I can only work with a couple of dozen people at a time, I thought of this book as a megaphone of sorts to help the tens to hundreds of thousands of people I'll never meet.

I've worked with 100+ founders and entrepreneurs, co-piloting this exact journey, where they are roller-coastering toward eight-, nine-, even 10-figure exits.

Multi-billion-dollar IPOs. THAT kind of wealth creation, which often happens when they are in their thirties and forties. And I've met *many hundreds* more along my journey. I'm going to share some stories, of course disguising any client references as composites to protect everyone's anonymity. I'm hoping many readers will laugh a bunch. And more importantly, think. A lot.

And I've lived the same journey as my clients. I co-founded a business that I sold a few years ago, when I was 46 years old. I, too, had one of those "step function" wealth creation events, which provided me with a firsthand and front-row perspective on what my clients are seeing and *feeling*. To contextualize, I often say that I'd be happy to get a call from myself if I were someone going through an exit. It wouldn't be the best call of the year, but it would be a pretty good one.

This first-person lens, coupled with my co-piloting, has created a unique vision into this world. Maybe even 20/15 vision.

The magic of "carries"

In these pages, I'm going to tell you not just how to change how you think about money but also how to stay grounded and connected to what really matters to you, so that you can enjoy and utilize your wealth to make sure your compass is pointing towards your True North along the way.

This isn't going to be a textbook-style read with to-do lists, exercises, etc. That's boring as shit (although for you boring folks, I do have some call-out boxes along the way that give you literal, non-creative, non-metaphorical versions of everything, as well.)

The *power* of this book lies in my frameworks. For decades, people in my personal and professional life have called these ideas a bunch of names, the most popular of which has been "Katzisms." For the purposes of this book, I've decided to call them "Carries," ideas that you can integrate into your life and bring with you on the rest of your journey. They'll be portable, pocket-sized tools you will always have handy. Some of the Carries, you'll digest overnight—especially if you're in the middle of a step-function, wealth creation event. Some, you'll be allergic to...until the moment when/if they are finally relevant to you. And some will take longer to assimilate into your DNA.

By tapping into the Carries, in everyday moments, you will likely find yourself making different types of decisions. Sometimes faster, and quite differently, than you had before. To make it intuitive, I've also grouped the Carries into four categories (and put a little symbol next to them as an easy-to-reference legend):

- Advice
- Money
- Mindset
- Career

There are at least two ways you can interact with the Carries:

1. You can read this book cover-to-cover and encounter them along the way, where I've contextualized them to when and where they were birthed.
2. You can leaf through the book, skipping my storytelling, and simply look for all the grey boxes with one of these four symbols. Inside of them, you'll find the "Why the hell didn't I think of it that way before I read this book?" stuff—the kishkas (i.e., guts) of this book. You'll be able to carry these ideas around with you, without anyone really noticing—until you take them out and the magic happens.

The next digit

This book is about digits. A LOT of them. Numerators. Denominators. Decimal points. Percentages. But in a creative "right brain" type of way. Meaning a more dynamic approach to numbers and the resulting math, when combined in unexpected ways that help empower and embolden those who embrace it. It's intuitive stuff. Won't call for a calculator. Won't require a protractor, although I use one as a visual later in the book.

Life, choices, decisions, and most importantly, and confusingly, the importance of various units of money changes when your wealth shifts to the next digit. We'll get into this more deeply, but it's weird when suddenly something that costs $5,000 shrinks to an almost invisible fraction of your wealth.

What if you're a millionaire (or a thousandaire)?

Over the past few months, when people asked me about the book I've been writing, I discovered that a wider variety of people than I originally thought are finding these frameworks helpful. So while I've focused on people already in the eight-, nine- or 10-figure "clubs," I believe that many of these concepts will have universal appeal to people with any line of sight towards serious financial wealth, whether it's making it to those levels or simply aspiring toward them, and that will allow the ideas to transcend many more wealth levels than I originally intended. So, regardless of which "club" you're a part of, I think you will find there is something here for you.

With that in mind, here is your first Carry, probably the most important one. Consider it the compass of all compasses to guide you through the rest of the book.

FINANCIAL WEALTH IS A GATEWAY, NOT A DESTINATION

The money. The net worth. The bank account. The financial wealth. They are not the destination. I repeat, they are NOT the destination. They are simply a gateway. To *real* wealth:

Time wealth.

Autonomy wealth.

Health wealth.

Without intention, inertial forces and habits will keep banging into financial wealth as the goal, and lead to trying to accumulate more and more.

Said differently, real wealth is getting up every day, doing what you want, where you want and with whomever you want. Without this mindset, people are unlikely to ever achieve real wealth and will keep trying to make their bank accounts bigger for no real or impactful reason.

Step into the Magnavator

My hope is that you'll read this book as if you're in the "Magnavator," a concept I came up with in my inventing phase as a kid. The Magnavator was a pod that could go in any direction. Imagine a Willy Wonka elevator car, where you are fully encased in a thick, fully encompassing layer created with an almost paint-like magnetic substance, so that the vehicle is always charged as a North magnet and the inside of the sphere is charged South. You can dial up the intensity between North and South so that you can travel from point to point, almost "flying" through the air.

Obviously, it's a ridiculous concept. Impractical. Interesting, but I'd imagine, fully defying the actual laws of physics.

But why do we *unlearn* how to think this way, the way we did as seven-year-old kids? Reconnecting with the zaniest parts of your imagination will help you if you've had a step function wealth creation event, or expect to someday, because you'll be entering a realm just as fantastic and unbounded.

Are you ready? Then, as my wife loves to say to me, "Buckle up, buttercup!"

PART ONE

DIGITS

CHAPTER 1

MELTING KEVLAR

0[1] The accidental client

People tend to find me by accident. They are often looking for someone who "can help a founder set up a trust before a liquidity event," or "manage their wealth after a liquidity event," or "meet some potential investors in their new startup" – stuff like that tends to prompt historical introductions. I can help with all those things for sure, but that's not actually what I DO for people at all. So, when they get connected to me and I pop onto a Zoom screen with my casual vibe, or meet up with them at a bar, it usually takes a good chunk of our time together to remember why they were even introduced to me in the first place. And that is fun. While I can address what they think they're looking for, that's the easy thing to identify. But they often come looking for one thing and find another.

0[2] Going off script

It's not that I'm *not* looking to help people with the thing they were seeking via the introduction. It's just that I know they're asking for a mechanism to help them achieve a goal that I have yet to learn. And

I never take it on a surface level that their self-identified route to that goal is the best one. So, I ask a lot of questions. Often in an order that is less obvious. I relate stories about similar things I've helped with. I ask about "what else" they spend their days doing. And I tell them a lot about me.

Inevitably, in a first 30-minute interaction, we'll touch on the "stuff" that prompted the intro, but it's naturally woven into the fabric of the conversation with context and often takes up less than 10% of our time. It's rare that it's the last conversation, so with that long-term time perspective, it's easy not to feel rushed.

Speaking of time and perspective, I often say that "time machines exist." Obviously, not quite the type of flux capacitor that needs a velocity of 88 mph. But in your head. Along those lines, it's crucial that I insert a framework (which I posted on Medium in 2014 under a pseudonym AKarmarang – as in "Adam Katz Karma Is a Boomerang mashed up") that explains HOW I played around with time and activity to create my business. It was a play on the classic "Important/Urgent," 2x2 matrix. The "give/help first" mentality.

I called it "Seed Planting versus Shaking Trees" back then, but now simply say "Seed Planting versus Tree Shaking"

"Seed Planting versus Shaking Trees"

September 1, 2014

Storming and Frameworks:

I'm an active guy by all accounts. I do a lot of "storming" in all areas of life (i.e., hyperactivity with no specific rhyme or reason to start with…I just "go.") But then have the discipline to juxtapose that with a systematic process for looking in the rear-view mirror to see what's going on behind me. Put excess capacity in front of me and I'll fill it up immediately. 30-hour day...would love to meet you! But all of this "storming" and systematic reflection creates FRAMEWORKS for lots of things in my life. My hope is to share ones that can be helpful to others. Because I find once the frameworks are in place, my go-forward plans have a lot more purpose and focus. "Seed Planting versus Shaking Trees" is one of my favorite frameworks that I've designed over the past few years and hope you find it helpful!

Full disclosure...while my days are spent in a business development function within the financial services world (i.e., private wealth management), I believe this construct is transferable into so many arenas!

Data Points and Valid Anecdotal Samples:

At some point, I believe you have enough data points to create a valid anecdotal sample...and after years of having 15–25 meetings a week (yes, that's ~1,000/year...exhausting to write, more exhausting to live), I felt that I had enough data points to create the "Seed Planting versus Shaking Trees" framework. Here is how it goes:

Shaking the Tree:

Most people who occupy my role (or any business development function) walk onto an open field and look for the healthiest-looking tree around, with the most abundant, plush bushel of leaves. This is not meant to be a direct metaphor, but let's just think of it as that money tree that my dad told me didn't exist in the backyard all throughout childhood. They sprint up to that tree...and they SHAKE it. A lot. And then they shake it some more. And repeat. If that doesn't work, they begin to throw things at it…maybe even try to cut off some limbs. Anything they can do to possibly get some of the green stuff off of the tree! That's how I first started, too. Luckily, I was a fast runner. Although, as fast as I was, many people were already at these trees by the time I got there. Hmmm…

Seed Planting:

Throughout my thousands of meetings, I started to identify pretty early on that I was meeting with two basic clusters of people. Those robust, towering trees that I describe above…and folks that weren't even a sapling yet. They were oftentimes on the other side of the proverbial field, not visible to anyone else, as they were simply seeds below the surface. No one was talking to them. As I met with the "seeds," I learned that they tended to have a relatively homogeneous set of needs that always surfaced and were front burner…but my "day job" and solutions that I had to offer were rarely one of them! So, I stepped back and realized that I was doing things all wrong…and was running the wrong way and in the wrong direction on that field. I'm no hockey fan (although my wife is Canadian), but I believe it was the great Wayne Gretzky who said he was so good because he always "skated towards where the puck was going." So…I started running fast…but in a direction where no one else was. There was no tree to shake in the direction I was running…no visible green stuff to shake loose…YET.

The Framework:

So, I realized that my role was all about figuring out how to be immediately helpful and relevant to those seeds early on, recognizing that my "day job" had little to do with what they needed. They needed water, irrigation, nourishment, sunlight, etc. In the real world, this meant capital, talent and business partnerships to accelerate growth. None of that was me, but it was absolutely my network and introductions that I could offer. By thoughtfully opening my network, I was immediately a source of help for the things they self-identified were important. Understanding this dynamic, I instantly transformed myself into the provider of that sunlight to survive. I was the conduit to that amazing water source full of nourishment. And suddenly, those planted seeds begin to grow into saplings…and eventually, healthy, plush trees.

But the difference is by helping to plant the seeds and help create the root system and the strong tree trunk…you are an important part of that tree. Of course, once it sprouts and begins to fill in with green leaves, everyone starts running towards it on that proverbial field. The difference in this scenario is that, as fast as they might run, I would be there first…by many years.

Perspective:

I always say in 2045, I couldn't care less if you're a client in 2014 or 2019. Who will even remember at that point? Along those lines, over the course of five years, you can shake a tree, and green leaves may eventually fall off. Or you can spend those same five years deploying and activating your personal network to serve as a pivotal lifeline to those seeds early on…and watch and help it sprout and grow over time into one of those plush, robust trees that everyone seems to crowd around. But remember, to the robust, plush tree that you are shaking today, you are an annoyance…and to the seedling-turned-tree, you are an essential part of the ecosystem that allowed it to survive and thrive.

Final Takeaway:

I spend no time shaking trees…only planting seeds, growing root systems and being part of the tree trunk. In a role that inherently gets rejected most of the time, I rarely do. It's simple. I spend my day helping people on the things they tell me they need help with. No one rejects help. But an amazing thing also happens over time. Lots of the folks I help shake those other trees for me.

SEED PLANTING VERSUS TREE SHAKING
IT'S SHIP DEV, NOT BIZ DEV

When looking to build a business, a customer base or anything similar, focus on what matters most to the people you are chatting with. It might be personal stuff, it might be business ideas, but, regardless, simply help them with what they are most focused on. It's their agenda, not yours. Build relationSHIPs, not BIZness. The "business" will simply be a result of authentic relationships built on a helping mindset, not the goal in of itself.

0³ The Venn Diagram

Most of the people I spend my time with cluster into a relatively homogenous part of a Venn diagram as it relates to two or three qualifiers: source of wealth (founders/entrepreneurs), stage of life (often single, or newly married...sometimes have a young child) and age (mid 30's-40's).

These folks are smart. They are inquisitive. They are used to being in charge. Our conversations are always a part of their day or week they weren't expecting. Their Kevlar exterior often thins quite quickly as vulnerability melts it away. I don't get the benefit of a white coat in a doctor's office, but I quickly create a safe space to allow them to drop their proverbial pants. I can always identify the moment when it happens. Different body language, softer facial expressions, an easier tone in delivering the information. That's when I know we are now *there*.

0⁴ Information asymmetry

Being an alpha all day long is exhausting. For many of these new acquaintances, chatting with me simulates a therapy or coaching session, and that's by design. I use different tools (no pharmacology or couches), just relatable frameworks for gnarly and scary stuff I figured out early on. I drag people way outside their comfort zone and educate them on the stuff that's out there. They quickly realize that it's *that* information that will truly guide their decisions, and they need me to navigate a space they didn't even know existed.

I always hold my two hands up and show them a visual. I start by keeping my hands static and very far apart. I explain that on the information spectrum, the higher hand is me, and the lower hand is them. And that gap in between is the information asymmetry that now exists between us. The asymmetry is palpable, and my goal in a long-term relationship is to narrow that gap substantially.

As I'm saying this, I'm purposely bringing my hands closer together. But not in unison. I, up there with the higher hand, stay static. I shrink the distance by bringing my lower hand towards that one. I explain that my goal is to teach, coach and educate, reducing that gap. I still always leave a little room, because I anticipate that I'll possess some additional asymmetry in perpetuity. And then, I move *both* hands up higher, together, maintaining the small, steady gap between us, but with each of us growing as partners.

My dad was a guidance counselor, my mom a speech therapist. The point of all this is that I'm an educator as well, and if we partner going forward, I'm going to need you to engage and learn so we can have participatory conversations, not one-sided lectures. This is an important part of my two-way interview, which is typically going on unbeknownst to them. They think it's a one-way interview, oddly, until they get to know me and realize it's not.

IT'S A TWO-WAY INTERVIEW

In every interaction, even if you "need" something, be discerning. If you are looking to bring on a client, customer or advisor, evaluate what you think of them, as much as they are evaluating you. Don't just do this at the beginning of a relationship, but throughout. The interview never ends. But remember, it should never be one-sided, regardless of what either side thinks. If you're not conducting your own two-way interviews on a rolling basis, you're probably missing something important.

CHAPTER 2

Tim

0^5 Preparing to "eject"

I met Tim, or rather, he "found" me eight years ago. Technically, he was already a client of my old firm. His parents had worked with us for decades. And when he came into some of his own money, he opened an account with us.

When a friend sent him my contact information, Tim noticed my auto signature came from the same firm as his advisors. This happens more than you would think, with more than 15,000 advisors at the firm. There was one crucial difference, however. My signature included the words "Private Banking". His family's advisors didn't.

Tim was confused, intrigued, and a little jealous. He wanted to be a private banking client. And his desire wasn't that simple.

At the time, Tim was a CMO at a high-flying direct-to-consumer fashion brand, but that situation was temporary. He had been screwed about a decade ago, when he started his first company in college. He was worth $80 million on paper in his late twenties. A major investment bank wanted him as a client. They got him, but by the time his six-month lock-up on that eight-figure stock position ended, the stock's value had plummeted 95%, and he couldn't sell it.

His assets were worth less than $1 million.

The bank burped him out as if he had the stench of a day-old opened beer can.

Why? Tim was no longer worthy of their club. Now he was looking for redemption. He wanted "in" to the club…our club.

Some people might have a negative view of someone who wants to be part of a fancy club for the sake of its fanciness. That's why most people who aspire to wealth will say that the destination is not the motivation; it's simply the outcome of the journey.

That's sometimes bullshit. Many motivations drive successful entrepreneurs. And I'd argue that wanting "in" to an elite club, a goal oddly demonized by society, is more than okay.

Tim shared his story with me as we got to know each other over the next year. My gut told me he had another big hit in front of him. He was smart. He was motivated. And though he was working for a hot startup, we both knew you don't create significant wealth working for someone else (or not usually). It was only a matter of time until he'd hit the eject button without a parachute and start his own company. This was going to be the startup that would enable him to get behind the velvet rope and into the fancy club that had eluded him for a decade. I was willing to bet on him.

0^6 Wristband envy

What Tim wanted was *the* wristband. Have you ever been to an all-inclusive resort or on a cruise and noticed someone, or maybe a group of people, wearing a distinctive colored wristband that no one else is wearing? Or waited for a beer at Yankee Stadium and noticed that someone next to you has a wristband that says LEGENDS on it? (Fair-weather fan over here; Dad grew up in the Bronx, and his anxiousness regarding traffic convinced me that baseball games only had seven innings).

The wristband could be one of those crappy plastic ones you get at the town fair (the one that a teenage kid, multitasking with their non-TikToking hand, wraps around your wrist like a newborn's ID tag and leaves the extra plastic dangling 5" too long).

The wristband could be a super-cool, pulsating one that instantly and unknowingly casts you into the full light show at a Coldplay concert (when you're looking to be seen, of course). Or it could be that special one that gets you into an exclusive place that most people don't really know exists—or, if they did, wouldn't really know how to get into.

In Tim's case, it was the rarified-air, exclusive, get-backstage-with-Taylor-Swift-and-have-her-laugh-at-your-favorite-jokes-and-want-to-take-selfies-with-YOU wristband. Special, unique, elusive–one that may not even exist...but the only way to find out is to get out there and start the hunt. Not the county-fair tourniquet, not the "light me up like a Christmas tree" concert prop.

That said, acquiring a "wristband" has many connotations, no matter how private you want to be. Often accompanying outlier success are family members and friends you didn't invite, Mr. Judgy and Mrs. Expectation.

"I wonder HOW they got that?"

"I bet they're a douchebag."

"How did THEY get one of THOSE wristbands?"

Managing these commentators in your own mind is the tricky part of achieving visible success, as he was going to find out.

0^7 Three commas, 10 digits

Tim had *done it before*. Post the expulsion from the major investment bank, he had started and sold a small business. That gave him a few million dollars, which had been sitting with his parents' advisor at my firm. While not a life-changing amount, it proved to the proverbial world and me that he was a winner and likely could do it again. Faster. Bigger. For his investors AND himself.

As I predicted, Tim left his CMO role at the DTC startup. He went to market quickly in his next business with a solution that wasn't far afield from his first successful company, but had a "TAM" that was making the entire venture capital community salivate.

But before we move on, can we talk about the ridiculous acronyms that businesspeople use in non-business settings, presuming everyone else learned them during some SAT-like prep course and that ridiculous acronyms are a universally understood language?

I bet half of the people reading this are like, "What the hell is a TAM? Is it a soda? Oh, wait! That was a TAB. Oh, Marty McFly."

TAM means Total Addressable Market. And this company's TAM was enormous.

Tim's product was a viral "must-have." Over the next seven years, he crushed it. The company had hockey stick revenue growth. He created a great team. And his company eventually got acquired for the Holy Grail B-word. THAT is the club he was looking to become part of. A founder with a billion-dollar exit. It has a name but also has two mathematically distinctive characteristics: 3 commas and 10 digits.

It's always fun for me to throw those monikers out in casual conversation and watch people bring out their trusty, high-tech 10-digit calculator (i.e., two hands and 10 fingers) to help figure out what 10 digits mean! See what we did there 😊)?

So, back to Tim. He was now, and forever, part of this elusive 10-digit club (well, personally, he "only" had nine digits, but he will always be known for his billion-dollar exit). He had arrived. His journey was complete. Or so he thought...

0[8] To help or not to help...that is the question

When you are prepping for a step-function wealth creation event, as Tim was, you can't help but dream a bit about how you're going to spend the money.

The dreams are usually not about a car or something under the audience members' seats. They go more like this:

"You get your mortgage paid off."

"You can pay for your kids' schools."

"You go on a crazy vacation."

And "You help your local YMCA get the playground redone."

I call these the "Oprah Moments."

The uncomfortable and unknowable part of this, for the newly minted club member, is how MUCH to spend, help and donate. Figuring that out will feel weird. It's a complex cocktail whose mixture and ratios take some time to get to taste just right. Sometimes your mixed drink may be a bit too bitter and full of envy; sometimes, a bit too sweet with gratitude.

Should you shake it, potentially causing unintended disruption to others' lives? Or is it better to stir it methodically, slowly and deliberately, integrating this money into other people's values and self-worth? It's important to think about the unintended consequences of helping others, which can arise if you don't explain your motives clearly.

JUDGMENT, EXPECTATION AND ENVY

Creating real wealth comes with stigmas. People will be jealous. They'll question your choices. Their internal monologue will say even more than their externally uttered words. It's life. Human nature. Expect it and do your best to head it off. Be clear with people about your "why" versus just letting them see your "what." Be direct. Absent communication regarding your motivations, people will create their own narratives. You also may simply not care, but don't pretend that it doesn't and won't exist.

0^9 Numerators and denominators

I love talking about numerators and denominators, both their relationship as a couple and their wild, alternative single lives. (My kids, ages 20 and 16, often wonder why they learn concepts like this in school, and you'll soon see why I tell them to pay attention).

When Tim was prepping for the sizing of his nine-digit club wristband, he was confused (understandably) about how to think about his new denominator of wealth.

So, I used a basic example. When Tim was planning his first celebratory vacation, I asked him what his family was planning to do. At this point, he had been married for 15 years and had two kids under 10 years old.

I could see the pride and excitement on his face as he started to tell me about it.

"How much will this whole thing cost?" I sorta stopped him mid-sentence.

"$40k," he blurted proudly.

"Oh," I said. I wasn't trying to be an asshole, but I did intend my borderline yawn delivery of that two-letter word.

I felt like I had literally taken out a safety pin and popped a gigantic Bazooka gum bubble all over his face, one so big I could barely see his head behind it. And when it popped, it was in his hair, dangling from his chin...that kind of scene.

Tim had been as excited as that little kid who finally figured out the pace and pressure to blow that face-eclipsing-gum-bubble. I not only burst it but also made him feel the same humiliation and shame.

I probably didn't quite anticipate the gum-in-hair-need-to-cut-it-out mess I caused, but I did want to spark a conversation.

Once he cleaned himself up, he shot back, "Umm, that's 2x more than I've ever spent before."

Now, remember, he had a reasonable-sized exit before and had about $6 million in the bank before getting this new wristband, so it wasn't like his prior vacations had consisted of him cramming a family of four into a 218-sq-ft internal room above the engine on a Carnival cruise.

But still.

He hadn't reoriented his relationship to money, specifically his new denominator. Money's value is relative to our net worth. Still, our psychological perception of it doesn't always change in proportion, a concept I call the "unitization of money."

Even if you've dreamed of a big exit or another windfall your whole life, going through a "step function" wealth creation event is daunting. I know, no one is panicking looking for their Puffs Plus (without the Vicks VapoRub...man, that stuff is disgusting, albeit my son craves it when he's sick. Btw, isn't it crazy how Kleenex, another brand I don't favor, somehow became the actual word for "tissue" to many people? Wild!) for people having massive windfalls of money, but it's a very strange dynamic. It has the potential to create a lonely and isolating life, unless you reframe your thinking.

Reorienting your relationship to money is challenging. Untethering your most formative memories of it is difficult. That umbilical cord to those nourishing years of money teachings requires not a scalpel but a bolt cutter of epic leverage and strength. Having been through much of this myself (and still experiencing it), I can tell you that this bolt cutter is not available at Home Depot.

So, with all of this in mind, I asked a few questions:

- How did you all fly?
- Where did you stay?
- How many rooms did you get?
- What restaurants did you go to?
- Were there any cool excursions or activities?

As he proudly answered these questions, I took it all in. And then I said, "Well, what would the $80k version of this trip have looked like?"

And he quickly responded, "Zero chance I'm spending 4x what I used to spend. I just spent 2x more than I have EVER spent – and you're still giving me a hard time?"

So, I asked, "Can you tell me down to $40k what's in your account with me right now?"

He quickly looked at me, visibly sorta annoyed, sorta amused. "No. You know I can't."

I matter-of-factly replied, "All good. What about down to $400k?"

He looked up and to the right, clearly trying to see if he somehow could find the answer in some hidden screen in his head.

"NO. I actually can't." With a closed-mouth smile as punctuation.

He clearly had gotten the point, or so he had thought, but I crystallized it for him in an easy-to-remember framework.

"If you are proving to me that this $40,000 sitting in your big, proverbial bank account has no utility, then I challenge you to think about *why* you are valuing it so differently in your vacation budget. I understand that it's four times your old budget and that it's even twice this most recent stepped-up budget. But it's still the same $40k. And if you can't even *see* it anymore in your bank account, it is providing you *zero* utility just sitting there. Whereas if you port that numerator over from your ginormous denominator—and put it on the smaller vacation budget denominator, it can provide massive utility. It's still the same $40k, but now you can *see* it and derive palpable joy by utilizing it."

That conversation was the first time I really started thinking about numerators and denominators. Whether together as a couple or apart as singles, numerators and denominators take on a life of their own. Sometimes, we talk about them in "relative" relationships (i.e., this costs 50% more than that or this is 10% the cost of that), and sometimes in "absolute" ones (i.e., this costs $100,000 more than that or I save $9,000 on this). (As an aside, why do they still mention on any financial news station that "the Dow was down 1,000 points today"? That's a numerator absent a denominator and meant something very different when the Dow was at 10,000 than at 44,000.)

To make this really come alive, I ask clients to envision a droplet of water in a:

- glass
- thimble
- teaspoon.

I ask:

"Can you see the water droplet in the glass?" … *Of course, not...*

"Can you see the water droplet in the thimble?" ...*Nope, still can't....*

"Can you see the water droplet in the teaspoon?" ...*Barely...*

Tim's answers were along these lines, and so are most of my clients'.

But before we move on, here is a quick example from daily life that may or not actually be the origin story for this framework.

A new ice cream shop opened up in town many years ago. It's subsequently already closed. It's a chain, so I'd simply imagine the franchisee mismanaged it versus the dynamic I'm going to highlight as my simple marginal-utility-of-a-dollar example.

Some friends started going and told me about it. But their description of the shop always ended with a version of, "It was pretty good, but zero chance I'm going back since they charge 50% more for an ice cream cone than anywhere else in town." So eventually I asked one friend, "How much are we talking about? "It's $6 instead of $4." So, I quickly asked him, "Umm, is the ice cream *better*?" "Well yeah, Adam, but it's soooo much more exp...." I'd blurt in, "And... how many times a summer are you going to get an ice cream cone?" "I don't know, Adam, maybe 10 times." "So," I said, "for $20 a summer, you're not willing to have a better ice cream cone every time?"

My friend never went anywhere else all summer – especially since he realized he had no clue how many twenties he had in his wallet but was oddly overvaluing that $20 for his entire summer ice-cream cone budget. Numerators and denominators are a funny thing.

So, back to our original concept of the water droplet we can barely see in a teaspoon: Why do we have a different emotional attachment to that droplet when, inside a glass or even a thimble, it is invisible and inconsequential, providing zero utility or quenching of our thirst?

If you're heading toward a step-function wealth creation event, this is an important question to consider.

MARGINAL UTILITY OF A DOLLAR

Once you hit real eight-figure wealth, the next dollar gained, spent or donated has a diminishing impact on your balance sheet. It's weird. But it's real. At some point, the utility curve flattens, and there aren't any nicer restaurants to go to, better vacations to go on, etc. As you tap out consumption, think about other places you can put those marginal dollars where they'll have way more value. It could be a donation. It could be helping a friend. It could be a tip for a waiter. Similarly, at some point, if you have decades ahead of you, the investment return doesn't matter that much. The extra 1-2% per year will make your pie bigger at death, but do you care?

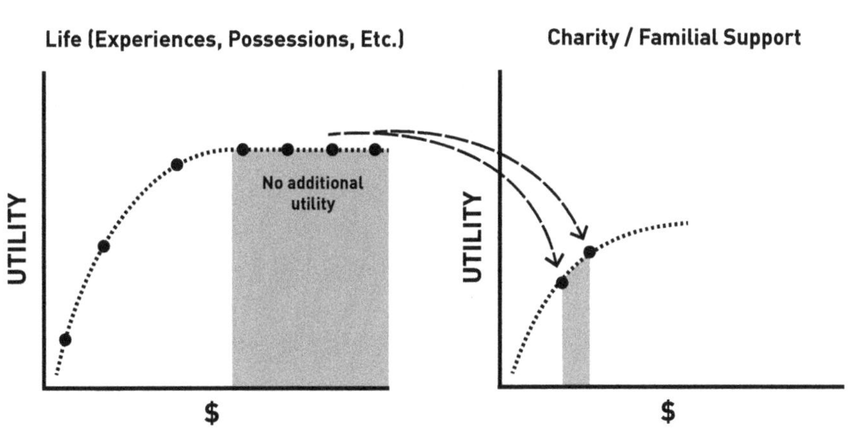

0^{10} Bank account bingo

So, this episode with Tim, and dozens like it, helped me home in on a related framework I use in daily life. When you close your eyes and think about your proverbial "bank account," can you do me a favor and tell me what's in it?

Don't be an asshole and be like "Adam, which one?" "Are you talking about my checking account, my brokerage account, my net worth?" I get it. How about this? Pick the biggest account for illustrative purposes. Nope, this isn't some weird magic trick. There's no listening device if you happen to say the number out loud.

I bet none of you could recite the amount past three digits from the left. Meaning, if you have $853,178, there's no way you knew more than $853, XXX or maybe only even two digits from the left: $85X, XXX. Weird, right?

And it doesn't stop there. If you have $8,531,789, I'd almost guarantee you said $8,53X, XXX or even again, only two digits from the left $8,5XX, XXX. Meaning you'd say out loud, "I have $8.53 million" or "I have $8.5 million." This doesn't stop. If you have $85,317,892, you'd say "I have $85.3 million" or possibly just the first two digits from the left, "I have $85 million." This matters because of what's to the ***right*** of all your first two to three digits from the left.

Most of what's to the right, uncomfortably, represents fancy meals, great sneakers, cars, vacations, etc.

THE 3-DIGIT RULE

No one knows their balance sheet more accurately than within three digits from the left. Most of the time it's even two digits. Be mindful of this. Think a lot about all the digits to the right. At eight-, nine- and 10-figure wealth, those "rounding error" digits to the right represent $100, $1,000 and $10,000 units. Most of daily life takes place in those ranges. Dinners. Donations for friends. Clothing. Shoes. Wedding gifts. The quicker you realize this, the less you'll sweat the small stuff, and the faster you'll enhance generosity.

PART TWO

WHERE IT ALL STARTED

CHAPTER 3

SHOP 'TIL YOU DROP

0[11] House of Gucci

There was no money tree in the Katz household. My dad rarely had any real cash in his wallet. First time I saw a $100 bill was in my junior year of college. My good buddy and I were in my room at a house I rented with friends. Most of them were in my fraternity. Recognize that I went to Brandeis. Undergraduate population of, like, 3,200. So, 800 to a class. Greek life was not really a big deal. Everyone knew each other even without belonging to a frat.

Anyway, this house was affectionately called the Gucci House. I DEFINITELY had no real clue as to why when I first moved in. I just went along. Not in that weird, lying, "Do you know what I'm talking about?" way of going along. Which, I might add, is a hilarious dynamic of our social fabric. Weird inertial insecurity dynamic of day-to-day life. When people say things and you have no clue what they mean, few people just say, "Ummm, slow down, what is XX or who is XX?" Anyway, I eventually realized that the name was inspired by a painted area around the whole roofline with the iconic Gucci colors.

The name still meant nothing, as I'd neither been in an actual Gucci store nor owned anything remotely like a Gucci product.

"Department store brand names for less every day." That Marshalls jingle was more the Katz family jam than this green-and-red pattern. Man, my memories of the dozens of trips there with my mom boil down to three pretty interesting ones. First, remember this is, like, the 1985-1989 era. I was the third child by a decent amount. We had no real disposable income, but Mom loved to bargain-peruse. Meaning I don't have much of a memory of her buying that much stuff. A pilgrimage to Marshalls might easily have lasted as long as our old family drives to Montreal from suburban New York. I mean, I feel like I was there for five to six hours at a clip. I don't think she fed me any snacks, or at least that I can recall. I had no iPhone, obviously...maybe eventually I had a Gameboy...albeit I can see her thinking that wasn't appropriate for me to have one. So, I'm guessing MOST of the time I sorta trailed around behind her, walked around the store by myself, etc.

0^{12} The ledge

There was no seating area at Marshalls. I mean, you're lucky if the changing area has walls (very diff from Syms, which we'll get to in a bit). But up front, near the checkout counters, were gigantic windows looking out to the parking lot where the Chevy Eurosport was collecting dust, given the length of our shopping trip.

Abutting the seemingly floor-to-ceiling windows was a ledge. Inside. It was brownish brick, from recollection. Not polished brick, but that old-school, jagged type that would catch any loose clothing or thread and pull them out to an irreparable length, ruining the calm weave where it had been nicely nestled moments before. And I wasn't very tall back then. I mean, I'm 5'9" on a good day as an adult.

So, let's just assume I was under five feet. And when I sat on this perch, my small butt barely fit on it, depth-wise. My quads extended out like a pirate ship plank, with a right angle into my lower legs and sneakers, cemented to the floor to keep me pushed up against the wall. It wasn't quite a wall-stand plank from martial arts class or boot camp, but it was more than sitting on a normal chair. Back up against the dirty window, sun usually beating on my shoulders through the glass, creating a greenhouse effect inside my shirt, causing what felt like an IV drip down my ass from my upper middle back.

It wasn't comfy. Well, because it wasn't supposed to be. It wasn't a seat. It wasn't a bench. It wasn't a sitting section. It was a windowsill. It wasn't meant for my scrawny ass and short legs. But it was my sanctuary. It was away from all the shopping. It was near all the cash registers and close to my eventual egress through those automatic doors adorned by my favorite four-letter word for the day, EXIT. I'd sit there for hours. Nothing to do. Nothing to play. Nothing to read. Just time to watch people. Think, daydream. Get mad at my mom. All good stuff. My ass would fall asleep. Go through the pain, then the numbness for a while. Eventually, I'd go find Mom and convince her it was time to leave.

That was probably my first experience with any form of negotiation. I was terrible at it. The worst was the on-the-way-to-the-cashier, last-minute, maybe-I-missed-something browsing she had to do. No matter what route I chose for us to get to the cash register, she'd find a way to "just double-check I didn't miss something" in pretty much every rack she'd just spent hours looking through. Remember, "Department store brand names for less every day" was playing in her head incessantly. Always on the hunt. So, eventually we'd make our way to the cash registers. All the cashiers sorta knew me at that point because I'd been creepily sitting on the window ledge for hours staring at all of them.

0[13] The checkbook

And now for memory two. I never really understood this. I mean, it's crazy that people still occasionally pull out a check in a grocery store line in front of me. But my mom LOVED the checkbook. She'd inevitably bust it out to pay for clothing at Marshall's. I think she even paid for manicures that way at the Nail Place (that was the name) when she'd go there every Friday. Clearly, she dragged me there, as well.

Btw, I have zero clue where my dad was during the Marshall pilgrimages. He didn't work on the weekends. My brother was in college. My sister was much older than I was. Maybe he was shuttling her around, or perhaps he was just home, sitting and reading. He didn't like sports much, except for the Yankees.

Weird that I was my mom's shopping buddy. I also used to watch *Days of Our Lives* with her at night since she taped it every day over the same VHS cassette. And we drank iced coffee, black, together. At night. It was leftovers from the pot she had made in the morning, from the Maxwell House tub-o-coffee (which was the same brand as my Passover Haggadah as a kid?!). Then she literally put the coffee in a jar in the fridge so that when it was time for us to watch *Days of Our Lives*, it was icy cold. No clue how I ever fell asleep with that much caffeine in my body at night!

0[14] Analog man

While we're talking about soap operas, let's go back to the pre-mobile phone era for a moment, to the parts of life that are now completely lost. Before cell phones, we all literally needed to call the HOME of the boy or girl we "like liked" – a la Kevin Arnold and Winnie from *The Wonder Years* – oh man, "Kevin Arnold has room in the crotch" might be one of my favorites and most used quotes from that era. Remember he's in what seems like a Sy Syms shop getting dress pants tailored for some event. He's up on that oddly-ubiquitous-6" high-carpeted-platform with his dress pants originally hemmed for a circus worker on stilts, where you put on some weird "dress shoes" so that the tailor could hem them. I loved that credit-card-shaped piece of chalk they all have. When I'd get my own pants hemmed, they made a line on one leg with the credit card chalk. Then they put in a few safety pins, and poof, they'd tell me I could get off the carpeted platform. As a math person, I always found it offensive that they just ASSUMED my legs were symmetrical in length. They always did just ONE.

Anyway, getting back to Kevin Arnold's episode and the platform. Most of the time, the tailors were just dealing with a hem, but sometimes they had to tackle the waist. I personally would always pull my pants to just above my hips. I'd have the eternal battle with my mom: "Adam Howard, pull your pants up over your belly button."

And then we'd inevitably have the fight in front of the other moms and boys: "Mom, I'm not wearing my pants over my belly button like Urkel."

"Well, that's where pants are worn, Adam." Seriously, same fight every time.

Now, unlike in Kevin's episode, they were never really dealing with the "seat" of the pants. Pants always fit well around my butt. But not for Kevin. He must have had a pancake-like-flat-ass which created space, the sag, and the inevitable, imaginary blurting across the store-wide loudspeaker normally reserved for discount proclamations, "Kevin Arnold has room in the crotch."

Even as a kid watching this show with my family (miss those days of live and scheduled TV, lost part of family life), I got the joke. Still to this day use it as a reference to lots of funny shit. Anyway, back to the HS dating scene and those dreaded calls to the girl's home.

So, you'd somehow get the boy or girl's number. I suppose they wrote it down on a piece of paper, or you had it in some school "directory," or you looked it up in the actual physical phone book that you had in some kitchen drawer. That last one was tricky because the phone number was always listed under the parents' name. And if they had a common name like Smith or even Katz, you'd need to triangulate the information with maybe a street you thought they lived on or something else.

Remember, this is all pre-Internet. You couldn't look up the parents with a search on LinkedIn or anything like that. So, it was hard to use the phone book as the primary source of the phone number.

0^{15} "This is Adam Katz. May I speak to Eve?"

So, when I got to my first job out of college, this woman in my group came up to me. She was like, "Adam Katz. You MUST be related to my 3rd grade teacher, Mrs. XX – don't recall the first name – Katz." I can't recall exactly where we were, but I walked her over to a telephone booth, pulled up the oddly thick hanging phone book, and got to the K's and eventually the Katz PAGES. I looked at her and said, "Katz is like Smith in this part of the country."

Funny how stuff like this happens. I forget where she was from, but to her, Katz was an unusual name. Phone books. Funny shit, just like physical maps.

So, anyway, back to the securing of the girl you like's phone number. Presuming you had the correct number, you were likely dialing it from a centralized location. Unless everyone was gone, you were dialing from maybe the family room, a den, but definitely not the central hub of the house, the kitchen. You probably at some point had the coveted "cordless" phone, which gave you the freedom, albeit limited to the shitty battery life of those devices, to call from your sanctuary of a bedroom. You'd dial the number and likely knew you'd have one of a few scenarios.

"Hi, Mrs. Smith, umm, this is Adam Katz. Is Eve home?"

Okay, it was the mom. They were usually pretty friendly and even took a trustworthy message with an accurate memorialization of your phone number for Eve to call you back because she was apparently washing her hair.

Then there was, "Hi, Mr. Smith, ummmmmmmmm, this is Adam Katz, can I speak to Eve, please?"

Ugh, it was the dad. The dad was the third worst scenario.

He's likely WAY larger than you, especially in your mind's eye. He's intimidating. But at least he's a grown-up. So, 50/50 he'll actually give his daughter, with a very clean head of hair, your phone number, and then another 50/50 he'll write it down correctly. By "it," I mean, your name AND your number.

And there's one other scenario.

"Hi, is Eve there?"

"Who's this?"

"Umm, it's Adam Katz."

"Does she know you? Are you from school?"

"I am Jim, I go to XX HS with you."

"Oh, right.... I have no idea where Eve is...think she's in the shower washing her hair. I'll have her call you back. Does she have your number?"

Now her big brother's last question was a gift. Most of the time, "call you back" was followed by a CLICK. Meaning, he didn't even ask for your number, presuming she had it. That was the worst. But, if he did ask, you know you had a REALLY low chance he got your name and number correct. In some ways, the CLICK was better because you could just pretend it didn't happen at all…OR you could be bold enough to call back later, "Just checking that Eve got the message," and hope you get Mom or Dad that time.

"Hi, umm, this message is for Eve. It's Adam Katz. Can you please have her call me back at 914-123-4567? Thank you"

The dreaded answering machine. Now this was a double-edged sword. In some ways, it's GREAT. You didn't have to talk to anyone. You got to say your name clearly, maybe even spell it after you said it if you were feeling thorough that day, and your number was stated clearly. BUT. The question is, WHO was going to pick up the message? Mom? Dad? Big Brother. The star of the show, Eve herself?

Oh man, if it were Big Bro, we thought he was likely going to make fun of the message to his friends and delete it. Reality is, he cared about the little guy chasing his little sis way less than we thought back then.

Last piece here before we get back on track. Answering machines. So, if you called my house, my mom thought it would be fun/nice to have a jingle for message leavers to listen to before the "beeeeep."

It went like this. My mom's voice (she died 15 years ago) is etched into my brain (and well, many of my friends,' too) with this message: "If a member of the Katz Family is the person you are seeking, please wait for the beep before you begin speaking. Just leave us your name and a number to call, and one of us will get back to you in no time at all. Thanks for calling." BEEEEEEEP.

So, I think the need to make that call to the girl's house is a lost art. But just think about how many speed bumps it put into the courtship of your crush. You had to speak to the parents and big brothers. You needed to leave messages with pre-pubescent vocal cords for the whole family to listen to when they got home from dinner, all huddled around the little machine with the cassette that was flashing the number "three." Meaning there were THREE people who had called the house. MAYBE one of the messages was for you. I remember standing in my dad's "office" downstairs, where the answering machine lived, with this exact answering-machine huddle. Paper pad with a pen next to it, to take down the messages. Even that created family bonding, like the live TV that is fully lost today. HS dating with no cell phones, answering machines and "room in the crotch." The 80s and 90s.

0[16] Shock and awe

Okay, getting back my Marshalls memories. Number three was Allison. She was a girl in my middle school. Really pretty. Dark hair, blue eyes. Super novel back then for some reason.

Anyway, so one day, I'm at Marshalls, as always. Older, so I guess roaming more than making my butt a potted plant on the jagged-brown-brick ledge. I'm walking down one of the actual aisles between the seas of clothing racks, seemingly parted that afternoon by divine intervention. The racks are relatively high, so I can't see around the corner. I'm just walking and thinking about nothing in particular. I turn the corner and there she is. I mean, THERE SHE FUCKING IS. IN MARSHALLS. With her friend Nicole, whom I sorta knew. I was in shock. I mean, not a real shock, but definitely one of my first real *holy shit* moments. I was surprised. So much so that one of my legs stopped functioning. I suddenly found myself on one knee. I wasn't proposing or anything, but I literally had one leg buckle in shock. I recovered quickly and bounced right back up into a normal middle school strut. I have no clue what we said to each other. We definitely talked a bit. But it was so formative. I remember thinking, "I can't believe she saw me in Marshalls!!!!!! FUCK." But then of course I had the realization that SHE was ALSO in Marshalls. Perhaps those pilgrimages weren't so bad in hindsight, minus the permanent dead-butt syndrome I still seem to have!

0^{17} Lycra

Okay, so back to the Gucci house. (Btw, I don't think they had any Gucci in Marshalls. At least none that I knew of.) So, there I am on the second floor, in my rented room. Still no clue as to why my folks let me live "off campus" in my junior year. The third-kid syndrome (no relation to the dead-butt syndrome) seems to be a catch-all for me whenever I'm curious about my parents' seemingly laissez-faire parenting…but nonetheless, I'm in my room and getting ready for a night in downtown Boston. I worked at a lot of the clubs, so I was usually able to get in pretty easily. I was going with a relatively new friend that night. He ended up being in my wedding party and vice versa, but I can't for the life of me remember how we met. He was in a different fraternity. Anyway, I remember us both wearing some type of Lycra top. That was "in" back then. I mean, it almost looked like a bicycle racing shirt minus the marsupial pouches on the back for drinks. He and I were rocking our shirts in some highlighter-worthy hues.

But the real memory was us both standing there, in front of the mirror, pulling up the front and showing each other our abs. Man, what I would give for what I affectionally now refer to as a "suburban four-pack." But the memory isn't that the poor overhead lighting didn't create the desired shadowing for our almost six-packs. Nor was it the Lycra shirts. Nor was it the actual evening.

It was the moment he took out his wallet a couple of hours before in his dorm room. He went into his closet and pulled out a wad (now in hindsight, I'm sure it wasn't an actual wad) of $100 bills. And there. You remember I'd never seen one when I came to Brandeis. I'm guessing that when he bought his Lycra shirts, he simply peeled a couple of those hundreds almost indiscernibly from his wad, way easier than he'd strip that shirt off after a sweaty night of clubbing.

Here is the weird part. And this is the most important observation. In my rented room with a mattress that was on the floor (no box spring, no bed frame, wasn't even my mattress), where I'd max out my dad's credit card by calling before a pilgrimage to Newbury Street, likely Urban Outfitters, dialing that 800 number on the back and listening for the golden words of "You have XX of available credit." And I'd spend all XX of it. At Urban Outfitters. For my tight Lycra shirts. Not to go bicycling. But to go clubbing.

But at that moment, when I saw the $100 bill, I can't imagine that my Shawmut bank account had more than $2,000 in it. That was the bank that had an ATM on my college campus, where I deposited my work-study checks from the coffee shop, which some think inspired the one on *Friends*, scooping Ben & Jerry's ice cream and making whipped cream from scratch, which once got in my ear during some foreplay and resulted in an ear infection.

0[18] Porting numerators

So, let's go back to the part where I was seeing a $100 bill for the first time, likely representing 5% of my own net worth back then. Extreme, but pretty accurate. So, again, think about when you saw that first $100 bill and what it MEANT to you. How it FELT to hold it. What it could BUY.

Now, let's play it out a bit more. Let's say you have $137,359 in one of your bank accounts today. Using my 3-digit rule, it's fair to say if you have:

$137,159
$137,259
$137,359
$137,459

In each of these scenarios, you'd like to simply say you have "about $137,000. Those $100 units aren't making it into your mental calculus anymore. You can no longer "see" that unit very much.

But let's now apply this to some other denominators of net worth, bank accounts, etc., and accelerate some unlearning of that formative memory of a $100 bill.

Let's say you have $1,373,594 in your bank account. Zero chance you know the difference, by heart between:

$1,371,594
$1,372,594
$1,373,594
$1,374,594

In any of those cases, if pressed to tell someone what's in your account, you'd say, "I have about 1.37 million," or possibly even "I have about 1.3 or 1.4 million."

Now here's where shit gets uncomfortable. You are rounding by $1,000 increments. And you can't even see them. Did your $100 "unit" now become a "$1,000" unit? Which is to ask, does the $1,000 now mean the same thing a $100 bill used to mean to you?

I can keep going, but you can see the POWER of the 3-digit rule. You start realizing that if a financial choice lives in some of these units, it uncomfortably matters less to YOU, but can impact so many amazing things.

You start porting these numerators onto other denominators, and magic starts to happen. Every time a friend is doing a marathon for charity, you give $1,000. Planning a vacation that might be $31,787 or $37,741—it oddly doesn't matter. It doesn't move the needle anymore. While many of us have never seen $1,000 bills or $10,000 bills, when you start thinking about the unitization of money, examples exist all around you. Close your eyes and begin to think about where and how to use them.

UNITIZATION OF MONEY

Related to the 3-digit rule, it's important to "own your units." Most people look at a $100 bill with a certain affection and assign it some grandeur. When you are worth $25 million or $250 million, I'd imagine your version of a $100 bill is actually a $10,000 bill or maybe even a $100,000 bill. Have you readjusted your mindset regarding your units of money? If not, start now. Understanding the unitization of money is amazingly empowering and will allow you to unlock the real value of your balance sheet.

CHAPTER 4

SIGNATURE STORIES

0[19] What the hell is investment banking?

I have a vivid memory of sitting in the family room of my childhood home during the summer before my junior year in college. It had that had plush, wall-to-wall, two-inch-thick brown carpet. I have fond memories from that era of watching in that room, the classic 80's show *The Love Connection*, with Chuck Wildebeest (as my Dad liked to call him even though it was Woolery), watching Chuck say "2 and 2 – be right back atcha" with the accompanying rotating hand gesture with two of his fingers held up, right before a commercial break. Formative memories indeed, especially in the non-fast-forward, non-on-demand era. You were actually forced to talk with one another during a commercial break.

So, fast forward a decade, and I am sitting on the couch, the second most-prime TV viewing area in the room, the smaller sofa my folks called the "love seat." I'm telling my parents about my girlfriend's friend, who has just gotten a job out of college, making $50,000 a year. This is 1997, and that was $2,000 more than my dad was making after working in the Bronx for 31 years as a guidance counselor!

My parents are taken aback, incredulous (not jealous or envious, just confused, given their life exposure until this point), asking me more about the job. I explain it is in something called "investment banking."

To be clear, at this time of my life, whenever I heard someone talk about "banker's hours," I always presumed the positive connotation that all banks closed at 5 p.m. I mean, it was later than Dad's school dismissal of 2 p.m., but "banker's hours" seemed good to me!

0^{20} The Yellow Pages

Fast forward a month or so, and I was back at my college. I picked up the Yellow Pages (again, 1997) and started cold-calling all firms, in alphabetical order, under the section called "Financial Services." Mind you, I was a psychology major in my junior year. I had taken zero math, economics or business classes.

Besides being a student, I was working at the campus coffee shop, Cholmondelys (pronounced Chum-leez), and also for a company that owned 19 bars and clubs in Boston. So, I was not exactly sitting on my ass doing nothing, but my efforts in those jobs massively outpaced and outshone my academic achievements. My grades were horrible. (I still to this day have that classic dream where I remember I have a midterm or final on the day of, and I haven't studied. For me, though, this isn't the classic nightmare, but an actual memory of several instances.)

Getting back to my pitch. If someone answered one of my cold calls, it was pretty straightforward:

"Hi, this is Adam Katz. I'm a junior at Brandeis University, and am currently the entertainment manager at our campus coffee shop and the concierge liaison at the Jaguars Group hospitality group, and I was wondering if you were looking for any interns this semester?"

In hindsight, not bad at all. Even as a 20-year-old with almost-drop-out-of-school grades, having a clear and direct communication style was instinctive and intuitive for me, and so was adding a few ways of saying things that were just a bit different to capture someone's attention.

Now, let's not dress up this activity the way I outfitted myself as the concierge liaison (i.e., I put on some ill-fitting sports jacket, a la the kid in BIG wearing Tom Hanks' suit, a bad tie and some non-denim pants). Then I walked into all the hotels in Boston, giving out my cards for them to send guests to the Jaguars Groups clubs, so I could earn $1 per card submitted with my name. Which was Kurt, because there was already another Adam at the company when I got there, and I thought Kurt was a cool name. That job was "pounding the pavement," while this internship outreach is "cold calling."

Both jobs sucked, but they were also a ton of fun. As crisp as my pitch was, especially delivered via the phone-sex-operator-worthy voice I was blessed with since I was 12 years old, it was still a numbers game. IF I got to the end of that full sentence pitch, in micro-machine-man-like record time, it was still usually met by an audible CLICK, and me saying "Hello? Hello? Are you there?" Or the more polite, "We aren't interested." But it was a contact sport. The more people you called, the better.

It took until I got the M's in the Financial Services section of the Yellow Pages of Greater Boston that I was met with, "Yes, we actually are looking for an intern. When can you come in?"

The company was called Merrill Lynch. In my mind's eye, this was a residential real estate firm. I apparently wasn't wrong; my information was just stale by like a decade or two. Apparently, Merrill Lynch had sold off this division a long time earlier. Driving through town in the back seat of my parents' Chevy Caprice Classic and pulling up in front of the building, I recall seeing those two names next to a picture of a bull.

Fast forward, and I got the internship. Well, of course I did! It wasn't exactly the most discerning interview process since it required 10 hours a week, and they weren't paying anything. This wasn't investment banking (I figured that out, maybe by the time the internship was over, months later), but it *was* Financial Services.

I remember telling one of my best friends at the time, who was pursuing investment banking for real at Dartmouth, that I got an internship at Merrill Lynch. He was like, "Umm, aren't you a psych major? And how the hell did you get that?" I explained how I cold-called and where the job was (downtown Boston, which required a one-hour commute each way on the train) and whom I was working for (a financial advisor named Bill), and he was like "Ohhhhh, you're working for a broker, got it."

I didn't really get the reason for his tone. He wasn't being a dick at all. He just had very different conversations on the couch with his parents through the years.

It was a world apart, but it was still one of the most recognizable brands in Financial Services, and I now had it as an attribute for the most important product (me) for the most important marketing project of my life: the creation of my first resume.

0^{21} 10 cents a minute

It was 11:01 p.m. one night in October 1997, and there I was, in my dorm closet (hard to call an 8'x10' space an actual room).

For those who grew up in that era, you know why 11:01 p.m. mattered. It's when "long distance" call rates switched over to the highly reduced rate of 10 cents a minute.

It was time to take out my one-pager that described this amazing new product: Adam Katz. And I was going to share it with the world, by feeding it into my 21st bday gift from my parents–a fax machine.

But let's back up a few months to discuss how this marketing presentation came to be, and more importantly, the lessons and learnings of how a kid from a non-target school with a 2.62 cumulative GPA, who got a ton of interviews and ultimately landed a sought-after job on Wall Street. In fact, 10 to 20 years ago, I thought that if I ever wrote a book, way before this book's contents were created, the title would be: "How to get a top job on Wall Street with a 2.62 GPA".

0[22] The pile

Envision 100 one-page resumes stacked on a recruiter's desk. If you were lucky enough to be second in that pile, the recruiter had way more energy than when they got to the 98th, or so I imagined.

So, my orientation was that this one-pager had to be universally appealing. If you think about the sections of a resume for someone coming out of college, they are typically:

- Education
- Work Experience
- Extracurricular Activities
- Interests

My view was that reviewers tended to gravitate to attributes that THEY often felt were their own highlights. Someone may have busted their ass staying up late to get straight A's, and associate that with a winner. Others might recall the two jobs they needed to juggle for 25 hours a week, and respect that type of grit and time management. Others might favor fellow athletes. And some might simply love quirky and unique interests. My goal was to make this document universally appealing regardless of which proctologist got the first look.

A few things stood out to pretty much anyone looking at my resume, regardless of my random birth order in the pile:

- *Isolating Right Brainers with Regard to Mathematical Applications and Manipulations* ("What the hell is that?" …but it sounds pretty interesting and smart!)
- *Competitive Arm Wrestling* ("Umm, does this kid think he's Sylvester Stallone? Is this even a thing? I will have to challenge him immediately when he comes in!")
- *Composition of Mathematical Poetry* ("That's the nerdiest thing I've ever heard of, and wow, can't wait to read one!!")

<u>Education:</u>

- Brandeis ("Okay, that's a pretty good school.")
- Major GPA: 3.3 ("Okay, that's fine, although not sure what classes are in his major that count.")
- Coursework: Economics, XXX, XXX ("Seems like he likes business even though he's a psychology major.")

<u>Work Experience:</u>

- Merrill Lynch and Smith Barney ("Wow, impressive…rarely see two internships from such national, recognizable names.")
- Cholmondleys Entertainment Manager ("Cool, he books bands, and something called a cappella groups and probably has to negotiate contracts, deal with payments, etc. Nice.") – remember this was way before the movie *Pitch Perfect* came out 😊
- Jaguars Group Concierge Liaison ("This kid is a hustler.")

<u>Extracurricular Activities:</u>

- Varsity track and field. Long jump ("Cool, he's a student athlete, check...but don't think I've ever actually met a "long jumper.")
- Student Sexuality and Information Service ("Yeah, I won't ask him about that but, for him!")

Again, underneath the sizzle of an unusual math brain and some freakish strength, I provided enough box-checking for the initial physical to get an excellent bill of health. I was universally appealing enough to get my resume pulled out of the stack for a conversation. But that was only the beginning. I didn't realize it at the time, but I had inadvertently cracked the code of resume building.

My resume appealed to people who were academic, creative, athletic, you name it... but the quirky stuff was pretty much all anyone ever wanted to talk about during my interviews. AND. That was what I wanted. It allowed *me* to dictate what I spoke about in an interview.

Now, listen, I'm not suggesting that your kids or the folks you are mentoring lie about anything. But I am asking that people think about how to creatively populate a universally appealing resume by tapping into the Magnavator recesses of your brain.

0^{23} Contact sport

I was at a workshop with other financial services hopefuls at the career center during my senior year. I knew none of them. None knew me. They were all econ majors. I had majored in psych.

A bunch of them were complaining they hadn't gotten any interviews. The career center team member asked them, "Well, how many resumes have you sent out?"

One kid said, "I think, like, 10."

Another "Maybe five or six."

She then looked at me, the random kid no one really knew, whom they probably thought was there to do a work-study thing in the Career Center. She was about to take out a gigantic vat of Kosher salt and pour it all over the econ majors' Grand Canyon-sized open wounds.

"Adam, how many have you sent out?"

"Not sure…maybe 150?"

The other kids: "Mmmmmmm."

"And Adam, how many interviews have you had?"

"Like 10," I replied.

Now, remember all the cold-calling I did for my first Financial Services internship and the pavement pounding I did for the Boston hotels? Trying to get a job is also a contact sport. You need to play in traffic to get hit. Use whatever analogy you want. It's a numbers game, and I had them. They didn't.

But then, when the resume sharing began, I had an epiphany.

All these kids didn't get it.

They had spent all of their time in college trying to get perfect grades in all of their classes.

But they missed the entire game.

Or maybe I was just playing a different one even back then.

They didn't realize that the singularly most important project they had in their entire college journey was to create a marketing pitch. The ultimate summation final exam. A one-page sizzle sheet.

And the product being marketed was THEM.

So, what I'm getting at here is that when you are sending your resume to someone, you have no idea of a couple of things. First, when are they going to take a look at it? Meaning, will they be energetic, tired, annoyed, hungover, etc.? You really don't know what kind of mood that person is going to be in. Second, what kind of person they are. (Not meaning an asshole or not. Although that is another dimension, I suppose.) I mean, what is their essence? What stuff do THEY give a shit about from personal biases? I don't mean gender, or race biases. I mean, biases towards people that are more like THEM.

Best way to think about this is "What class superlatives did they win in high school?" Were they voted "Smartest?" Well, if so, they may REALLY value grades and standardized test scores. Were they voted "Most Versatile?" Good scores, a "joiner" of clubs and maybe a sport or two? Then they probably care a lot about well-roundedness in life. If someone was voted "Most Athletic," they might really find it awesome if you played Varsity soccer for four years, were All-State and got a D1 scholarship. These are clichés, but it's easier to use buckets to illustrate my point.

Since you never know when a person is going to look at your resume, their mood or the way in which THEY spent their formative years, it's best to try to make your resume appeal to everyone. Especially if you're in the earlier parts of your career, think about the main sections:

Academics: Obviously, if you have amazing grades and standardized test scores, that helps. But think more creatively. Look back at my resume, and you'll see I created a math test. Who does that?! But it appealed to anyone who was into academics, a lot more so than my GPA in my major.

Work Experience. Do your best to get some type of internship or job in a related field. Or a recognizable name. And if not, be mindful of the *type* of work you were doing there and how you write about it. Remember, "skillsets" are transferable

Extracurricular Activities. I know, this disappears from our resumes as we get further into our careers. But people *love* talking about affinity stuff, leadership stuff, team stuff, etc. Make sure you've got something for everyone here!

Interests. Don't put the reader to sleep in this section. WAKE THEM THE FUCK UP. Meaning, it's the last section. It's a throwaway for most resumes, so you have the opportunity to FINALLY distinguish yourself with things that are uniquely you. It might be the *only* section in the *entire* resume that will differ from anything they've ever read. When I receive resumes today, I always read lame shit like running, hiking, piano or travel. Literally. Generic and boring as hell.

Compare that to mine: Competitive arm wrestling...composition of mathematical poetry. No one who read my post-college resume had *ever* seen either of those as interests...and if I'm wrong, and they had seen them, for sure had never seen them *together*. At least be descriptive if you can't be creative: "group fitness class addict," "hiking – 3-5k elevation," "80's music lover," or "adventure traveler."

THE UNIVERSALLY APPEALING RESUME

A resume is a marketing tool. You are the thing being marketed. Be smart. Be authentic. Don't be mundane or generic. Content, skills and knowledge are table stakes. Make sure each of the traditional sections includes elements that will catch a reviewer's eye. Show who you are by putting in unique "interests" that reveal your value system, how you think and where your passions lie. AI may soon make all resumes obsolete, but no matter what form they take in the future, one tenet will always hold true: At every stage in your career, people will ultimately want to work with people they like.

0^{24} Popping so many cherries at once

"His palms are sweaty, knees weak, arms are heavy..." That whole thing was sorta going on during the first interview in my senior year in college, as if it were a rap battle, not simply an interview, though it might as well have been, minus the vomited spaghetti on my shirt. In hindsight, this was certainly my first experience with what a lot of people call "imposter syndrome."

To set the stage, about two weeks earlier, I used the one and only "connection" of any sort that my family had. The daughter-in-law of one of my parents' best friends worked in college recruiting at Prudential Securities. Back then (again, 1997-era), they apparently had an investment banking division, which seemed strange at the time (albeit I was still searching for Merrill Lynch real estate listings).

"Welcome to the Rock." I still think of Sir Sean Connery whenever I go see the Devils or UFC and pull up to the Prudential Center.

Back to my rap battle. So, I had somehow parlayed a couple of "informational phone interviews" into an invitation to a "Super Saturday." As the name implies, it was on a Saturday, clearly providing a preview into what your life would look like as an investment banker and definitely not the kind of banker's hours I had envisioned back on the sofa of our family room.

But that word preceding it, that "super" part, left a lot to interpretation. Maybe like a "super set" at the gym, where you did a ton of different exercises for the same muscle group? But it was definitely not adjacent to other definitions of "super" in the dictionary.

Anyway, the first "imposter" moment was when the black car pulled into the driveway of my childhood home. My parents were like, "Umm, who's in the driveway?" I said, likely muffled through my "imposter" mask, "Oh, I guess that's the car to take me to NYC for the interview."

Mind you, I had never been on a plane with my family at this point in life (or ever since), and we definitely did not go to the elusive destination called an airport in a "black car." Back then, it was the super-ugly Lincoln Town Car that they recently resurrected in *Mayor of Kingstown* for Mike McLusky to drive (great show and even better car choice). But there it was, backed up in my driveway, trunk open, in front of my parents' Chevy Caprice Classic (may or may not have been the same one that I cruised around in, spotting all those Merrill Lynch real estate signs a decade prior). My folks were again confused. Not envious. Cautiously proud.

So I walked out with some form of an overnight bag. Remember, we didn't really go on trips, so I'm not really sure what overnight bags we had—and undoubtedly didn't bring my hard-cased sleep-away-summer-camp trunk. Back then, people were all suited up and with ties. In fact, I'm pretty sure I had to go with my dad for an emergency visit to Syms. He knew about the interview, but not the "black car."

For those who have never been to (or even heard of) Syms (as in Sy Syms), it was a battlefield for discount clothing. Sorta like Marshalls, they had their own slogan: "An educated consumer is our best customer." You never knew what you might find in the racks at Syms, which were nicely organized and easy to navigate. The area that always gave me a chuckle when we walked in was the "portly" section. That wouldn't go over well these days, but the name was an oddly accepted way of signaling to someone with less-typical waist-to-shoulder measurement ratios, that this section was upon you.

The most unique part of Syms was the dressing room. It was "prison shower meets the local JCC locker room." One large open room with benches around the perimeter, all facing inwards. You were pretty much forced to look at one another as you got undressed, tried on suits, showed them to your dad or someone else who was sent into the shower with you…and then decided if the suit looked good. Next, you would be marshaled out into another common room, with a little Kevin Arnold stage where you could display your newfound uniform and check yourself out from all angles in one of those tri-fold mirrors, somewhat like the similarly era'd suntanning trifold.

What were people thinking with those? Someone should have had the etcher write, "Frying skin may cause cancer," sorta like how car mirrors have signs warning, "Objects may be closer than they appear."

0[25] The ride

So, I packed my overnight bag with my Sy Syms suit inside, and on to New York City we went. While my dad worked in the Bronx for 31 years, and by definition literally went to the city five days a week for all of them (minus awesome summers off when he worked at my sleepaway camp, which required that hard-sided trunk I felt would be overkill as an overnight bag for the city), we pretty much NEVER went into New York City as a family for anything. I mean, I can count on one hand, with one of my five-digit calculators, how many times we made the trek when I was a kid.

Reflecting, it stemmed from the same theme that led to the seven-inning Yankees game in the Katz household: traffic. And stress from traffic. And stress from thinking about that traffic, that you were 100% going to hit it BOTH ways. Sadly, I inherited that same stress, as my family will attest to this day. Ask them about "airport Dad" or "end of concert Dad."

So, about an hour later, we arrived at the Millennium Hotel in downtown NYC, right near the former Twin Towers. Again, this was NYC in 1997. The landscape was quite literally and figuratively different.

I checked in at the front desk, where they already had my name, and then it came:

"Mr. Katz, your room is on the 20th floor. It has a beautiful view of the World Trade Center and the river. The room has already been paid for, and you also have a credit of $75 for dinner this evening and $25 for breakfast tomorrow morning. Enjoy your stay."

Ummmmmmm.

I was already confused. I hadn't even gotten the job, and they were telling me, Mr. Katz, that I could have $75 worth of room service, the part of the hotel stay that I didn't think was something ANYONE ever participated in. It was a thing of folklore in the Katz house.

What is this "room service" thing you speak of?

Again, during past hotel/motel visits in my life up until then, I didn't feel bad for myself because I didn't think any suckers would ever actually pay $18 for a hamburger, or at least that's the way it had been ingrained in my brain by my parents whenever we'd enter a hotel room. AND $25 for breakfast? What kind of chickens were laying $17 eggs...?

It was the morning, about an hour before my Super Saturday experience. I was still digesting last night's cart-delivered French Onion Soup, the Millennium Cheeseburger with Fries, and the Ice Cream Sundae, when I again pressed the Room Service button on my landline hotel-room phone, greeted now for the third time in less than 24 hours with a "Mr. Katz......"

Still weird to hear.

And still full from six hours earlier, I, of course didn't want that $25 to go to waste. At that point in life, I literally had a bottomless pit-style stomach embossed with a six-pack.

I often complain at this stage of life that my parents seemed to have ordered me a mini-bladder when they filled out the Chinese-restaurant-styled genetic-code scantron. Still, back then I humbly bragged, before the humble brag was en vogue, that my parents had opted for an "endless stomach" as a result of the same No. 2-pencil exercise they conducted in 1975 when I was conceived.

So, the French toast and eggs seemed like a nice complement to some chocolate milk. And with a packed stomach, a packed overnight bag, and a packed brain and heart, I made my way out of my 20th-floor palace, down the ear-popping elevator ride, through the nicest marble quarry (i.e., lobby) I'd ever seen in my life—and strutted a few blocks over to a huge building with Prudential Securities adorning its own quarry.

0^{26} Sizzle reel

Eight-interviews-in-a-row day. Why couldn't they just call it that instead of dressing it up like a concierge liaison and calling it a Super Saturday? It was weird.

I started the day asking a ton of questions in my first few interviews. They were all 30 minutes, so we couldn't get into much substance, but I noticed a pattern emerging: everyone wanted to ask me about my sizzle topics.

Arm wrestling.

Math poetry.

And so many questions about right-brain versus left-brain thinkers.

That was pretty much all anyone would ask me about. Nothing about finance. Nothing about my grades. They seemed not to even really care about their brethren, Mother Merrill, and that place where "they made money the old-fashioned way, they eaaaaarrrrnnnned it."

They seemed only to want to talk about these almost Ringling Brothers oddities. And I crushed it. They were reading my math poems about parallel lines and taking the math test that I created to ferret out the "right brainers." My Imposter Mask had been trampled and was unrecognizable; replaced by the Rock logo on my forehead, with Sean Connery in my ear.

Another thing also started to happen.

While THEY were working on MY math test during MY interview, I'd ask them a lot about their typical day, what they felt had made them successful, what they look for in a new analyst like me, etc. I pretty much learned from those first three interviews EXACTLY what to tell the next five interviewers.

So now, not only did I have all the sizzle, but I also told them exactly what they wanted to hear, by simply paraphrasing what their prior three colleagues had told me to say.

This skill and thought process was innate to me. It almost seemed like an odd, rigged system that I, the kid without the map to the airport or a proper overnight bag, figured out in about 1.5 hours.

But then it happened during the last interview of that Super Saturday.

"What is your cumulative GPA?"

I was barely sitting down yet when the MD uttered that five-word, novel phrase. (The MD was not a doctor, apparently, but a species called a managing director, a foreign title to a psychology major.)

I replied, "Umm, my major GPA is a 3.3."

"Oh, I can see that right here, but what's your cumulative?"

I scoured the floor and my pocket to find the clearly too-hastily-crumpled-up Imposter Mask and put it back on my face.

"2.62," I mumbled, barely audible.

He wasn't distracted by arm wrestling or math poetry. In fact, he never even made it past the Education section of my one-page marketing masterpiece. He was a one-dimensional thinker.

He subscribed to a specific flavor of standards. I was not a universally appealing candidate to him. And the Super was drained out of that Saturday immediately as he said, "How the hell did you make it to my office?"

I obviously didn't get that job, but I acquired so much more than I would have ever known.

0^{27} B'shert

At one of the many engagement parties my wife and I attended, the host gave us T-shirts that had a 5x10 subpar, pre-digital-camera-and-iPhone-era photo of us, printed with the words "B'Shirt" underneath this. It was a play on a Yiddish expression "B'shert," or "meant to be."

My wife and I had met only six or seven months earlier while on vacation. She lived in Montreal; I, in New Jersey. Only had four days there in common.

The concept of "B'shert" is simple but has played a role in many pivotal moments in my life. A couple of months after the eighth interviewer at the Rock stripped me of my logo tattoo and my Sean Connery accent, I made it to a Super Saturday at Merrill Lynch. It was not for Investment Banking, but instead for the Private Client Development Program within their Private Client Group.

Again, I didn't really know what that meant. However, Bill, the guy I interned for, was part of the Thundering Herd (that's what marketers thought was a good way to describe the army of brokers that brought Wall Street to Main Street at Mother Merrill) that was apparently wrangled within this group, and it seemed pretty interesting.

I had been told a week earlier that they were up to their second batch of 24 hopefuls for their program and that I was going to be part of the third batch, IF they didn't find enough candidates the following week.

Their Super Saturday was on a Tuesday, but I recall they still called it a Super Saturday, which is even stranger now as I reflect on that almost 30 years later.

So, I was in the Science Center at school when my Radio Shack phone rang. It literally said Radio Shack on the phone. It was pouring out, so I had probably sought shelter there—I can't fathom why else I would have been there as a psychology major.

I'd somehow procured a cell phone with zero credit. My parents didn't even have one. I think my brother, nine years my senior, still has one that was in a little duffle bag case you'd carry around, not quite like Zack Morris or Gordon Gekko's, but still a very cumbersome device.

Digression.

So, my butt was vibrating in the back pocket of my Lucky Jeans (they actually say "Lucky You" when you open the fly), where my mobile, job-seeking command center resided.

I pulled it out, extended the flimsy plastic antenna the full four inches, and saw a "609" area code. I knew this was Plainsboro, NJ, where Merrill Lynch is headquartered.

A nice woman named Nancy asked, "Is this Adam?"

She quickly gets to the point:

"I have good news for you. Someone dropped out of our Super Saturday, and we'd love to give you the spot. You've been persistent in following up about your candidacy, and we'd like for you to come to this cohort rather than waiting until the third one in a few weeks. Can you make it?"

And off I went to pack my Syms suit in my overnight bag and jump in the back of another "black car" on the way to Logan Airport (which I had also never been to, as Amtrak or a car was my mode of transportation between my hometown and college in Boston).

What if I hadn't been persistent? What if I hadn't gotten a cell phone? What if it hadn't been raining, and I sought refuge in a dry place when she called? What if, what if? It was an amazing reinforcement of so many things I hold dear to my personality and success. But again, it simply was B'shert.

0[28] Basic training

About 48 minutes after takeoff, we landed in Newark, NJ. Man, that was WAY better than Amtrak. Then I really arrived. A man in a suit by the baggage claim held an 8"11" piece of paper that said, "Mr. Adam Katz."

An hour later, we pulled up to a very elegant-looking building in downtown Princeton, NJ. I had never been to Princeton or to a hotel like this. It made the Millennium in NYC look like a tall Holiday Inn. Now, this place was fancy. So many things and people I had never really seen before. Who knew so many hotels had internal hallways?

The Private Client Development Program I was interviewing for was a management training program for different areas of the broker army. Weird that they were interviewing kids straight out of school for "management" jobs, but that's what they did back then.

Apparently, before they fancily renamed it the Private Client Development Program, they used to call it the "JET" program. PCDS definitely didn't roll off the tongue like JET.

It took me about five years to realize it wasn't "jet" as in "super-fast ascension and speed through management" but simply an acronym for Junior Executive Training. Acronym soup again—definitely not as tasty as my four-cheese soup from that Monday night.

So, the PCDS had a brochure. Meaning, it was a glossy, oblong "look book," showing some of the past alums and all of the 1997 class.

When we got there, that was part of our welcome kit for the Super Saturday on a Tuesday. Again, the script began: "Hello, Mr. Katz, you will be here for two nights with us. We have you in a beautiful room facing our garden. Your stay has already been taken care of, and all the meals will be with your group, except this evening. You have a $75 credit for dinner. Enjoy your stay."

I quickly looked through the agenda for the day, which was also included. The agenda was clever. Unique. The kryptonite to my "sizzle" strategy:

- 9:30-10:00 a.m. – Introduction to the program welcome
- 10:00-11:00 a.m. – Group interview
- 11:00-12:00 p.m. – Extracurricular activities interview
- 12:00-1:30 p.m. – Group lunch
- 1:30-2:30 p.m. – Work experience interview
- 2:30-3:30 p.m. – Academic interview
- 3:30 p.m. – Shuttle back to the hotel.

I had a variety of reactions and emotions.

First, for the agenda. Crap, how am I supposed to distract someone during a 60-minute interview solely focused on academics? Next, when looking at the brochure:

1. This is really fancy paper stock.
2. I can't believe they created this for this program.
3. Holy shit, most of the kids from this year's program went to Ivy League schools.
4. Most importantly, *I will be in the 1998 brochure.*

To this day, I can remember the taste of that $26 bowl of four-cheese soup. It was the most delicious thing I'd ever consumed. That was Monday night.

0[29] The group interview

Broken into some random, not-so-random groups of eight for this exercise, we sat in a circle of chairs, reminiscent of what a 12-step support group meeting looks like. I can't for the life of me remember the actual exercise. The only part I do recall was that they asked everyone to share something about themselves that no one would know by looking at their resume.

Most people's one-pagers were pretty pathetic, so there wasn't much inspiration from what existed there. The stuff that didn't even make it onto the resume was even less impressive. Luckily (for them), I didn't go first. I was maybe third. After hearing things like, "I'm really into science fiction novels" and "My family has a house in Aspen" (not sure what this place Aspirin is?), I blurted, "I know 75 digits of Pi by heart."

I saw it happen again. It was like being back at the career center when people heard I had faxed over 150 resumes. The other interviewees sort of chuckled, sort of looked down, and above their slouched and defeated bodies, I saw the three interviewers' heads perking up with large smiles. It was the first interview, but I knew—I was likely getting a wristband for this club.

SIGNATURE STORIES

At every stage in life, you'll have stories you tell friends or colleagues that convey the essence of who you are, what makes you tick, and what's on your mind. How you navigated the sale of your company recently. The failed launch of a new product. Your weight-loss journey. The Ironman half-triathlon you're training for. A new hobby. Be prepared and think actively about the go-tos you'll share as you get to know people. These should be easy to remember. They will and should change over time.

0^{30} The group lunch

I was going to fast-forward to the academic interview, but I need to do a virtual and figurative pit stop at lunchtime for a few reasons. I'll start by setting the stage: It required a walk down several window-adorned hallways, both long and wide, to a place called The Willows. Back then, Merrill Lynch's campus in Plainsboro was part office building, part hotel, and part conference center. And in the heart of it was, quite literally, a nice hotel-lobby-like restaurant called The Willows.

Again, this was another first. I pretty much went to three restaurants as a kid: the local kosher deli (no, no one in my family has any connection to the famed kosher "style" Katz's Delicatessen), the local diner (what a great Northeast invention!), and Hunan Teaneck (again, my family was kosher, and this was the Chinese restaurant we'd drive to about 40 minutes away in Teaneck, NJ).

The Willows was oddly fancy. Proper. It had the multiple sets of cutlery Vivian tried to figure out in that iconic Pretty Woman scene. I was a way shorter, less attractive version of her. No airborne escargot incident for Mr. Katz, but the four-course meal was definitely a learning experience.

Many of the interviewers seemed to eat there multiple times a week, based on the waiters' and waitresses' knowledge of their children and grandchildren, intermixed with the order-taking. The real, formative piece was that there were some celebrities interspersed at each table, some of whom were members of the 1997 brochure I had been studying since I got my welcome packet. Several clues made it obvious they were not part of our group. Confidence. Better-fitting clothing. Smaller cell phones.

The most B'shert part of that meal was meeting a 1997 celebrity who would become a lifelong friend and mentor. I didn't know then that Ed would be the one who, during a fateful conversation where I thought we were there to discuss my becoming a managing director (the alternate MD), redirected me to essentially leap off the management corporate ladder that I had been climbing for the past decade, essentially into an abyss. No safety harness. No trampoline-type net.

The trajectory of this imaginary leap. One where I'd essentially go flying down off the ladder, with the hope of landing in some type of chute that would propel me up and out of some trough, helped me visualize and actualize the common and less-discussed trajectory of the entrepreneurial journey I was about to embark on. I realized it looked like a hockey stick. Just not an ice hockey stick.

ARE WE PLAYING ICE OR FIELD HOCKEY?

When people make life and business decisions, it's important to understand the shape of the possible outcomes. Rarely is it a straight line up and to the right. I'd also offer that it's rarely an ice hockey stick. If it were, everyone would do the same thing. Meaning it's flat line until it starts going up and to the right. No "sacrifice" from your starting position other than perhaps perceived opportunity cost. But alas, the field hockey stick. It's shaped more like a "j." With private equity and venture capital, people are familiar with this shape of return outcomes. However, I don't believe people view this as a potential shape of life decisions, especially when it comes to careers and businesses. This isn't a good or bad thing, but it's important to be mindful of the shape of the curve. And if it is indeed a hockey stick, consider the question, "Are we talking ice or field?"

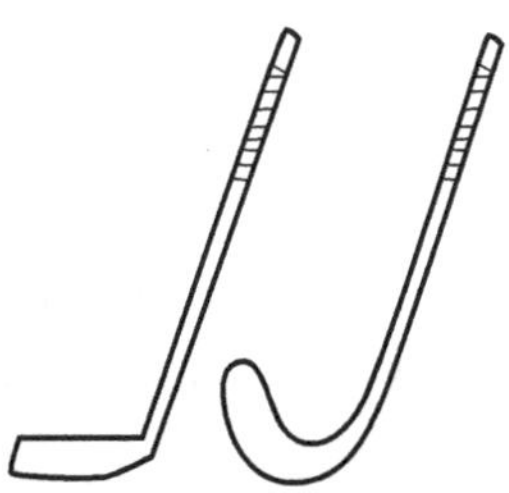

031 The academic interview

But we're getting ahead of ourselves. What was immediately ahead of me was the academic interview. Which was, yup, 60 minutes. That's how much they carved out to talk about just my academics. I sat down and recognized my interviewer. He had been one of those perked-up heads, curious about my math geekdom that shone on March 14 every year. I relaxed, and he looked at the shiny thing.

He asked, "How do you know 75 digits of Pi?" and I explained:

"Oh, well, while I was in an extra math class [see what I did there already?], I had finished a lot of the work more quickly than anticipated [again, doing the same thing], and I noticed that around the perimeter of the room, higher than the chalkboard, was a printout of numbers that went around three walls. I realized quickly there were a lot of digits of Pi. So, I thought it would be fun to memorize them. I simply chunked them into groups of 10 digits, like phone numbers, and it took me about 15 minutes to have them all memorized."

I guess in hindsight, that was probably a mic drop moment, but I didn't realize it. I mean, I sorta did, sorta didn't.

Then I said something to the effect of, "Since we're talking about math, would you like to read some of my math poems?"

That took a good 10 minutes. I was explaining to my interviewer how parallel lines adorned by a transversal a slight bit less than right can create intersecting lines, equating them to lovers… ya know, normal stuff like that. 😊

Then, as we got through the second or third math poem, I naturally transitioned to, "Do you know if you attack math from the conventional left brain or in a more creative way, from the right brain?"

He looked at me blankly and said, "I have no clue, but I'd be interested in finding out."

And then, for the next 20 minutes, he was taking my math test. I "graded" it for about 5-10 minutes, and we surmised he was a conventional left-brainer, like most people.

And then the interview ended.

I recognize that didn't exactly add up to 60 minutes, but let's assume we weren't exactly robots and there was some foreplay and small talk. I had gotten through the entire academic interview, and never was the question uttered, "What is your cuuuuuuumulative GPA?"

In fact, he never even asked about any of my grades, my classes, or even what my major GPA was.

I had distracted him.

I had shown him the shiny thing.

It was me.

It was academics, for sure—just not what he was anticipating, and not how any of his other interviews had gone that day (or maybe ever).

BACKWARDS MAZES

In any conversation, look ahead to where you want to go and work backwards. Think of a maze from your childhood. They were easiest to solve backward. Don't lose that skill, and use it often, in a sales meeting...an interview...a car or home negotiation. It will likely make the path forward much easier, more enjoyable and absent many dead ends and roadblocks.

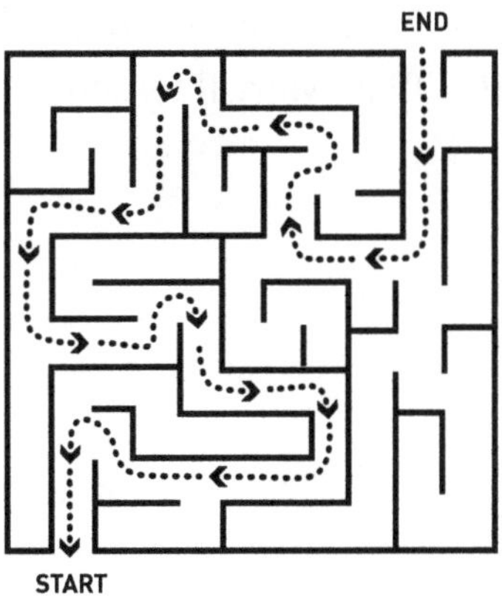

0[32] The call

So, I forgot to mention: the way this "Super Saturday on a Tuesday" interview process worked is that you arrived on Monday night via "black car" at the Princeton hotel.

You had your fancy room service. Went to sleep. Took a bus to your full day of interviews.

Then, back to the hotel with another $75 stipend for dinner/drinks.

Next came the crazy part: Between 7:00 a.m. and 7:30 a.m. on the next day, you got a call to let you know:

a) If you had been accepted into the 1998 brochure.

b) What role and location you got.

And—

They phoned the people granted "celebrity status" first.

Soooo, you pretty much knew if your phone didn't ring by the estimated 7:10 a.m., you didn't make the cut.

My wristband was delivered at 7:04 a.m.

The cold calling of financial services firms. The trekking from hotel to hotel, handing out my Kurt cards. The 21st birthday fax machine. And most importantly—the one-page sizzle piece. They finally got me a spot as the newest product to be marketed in a new medium—the 1998 PCDP at Merrill Lynch.

PART THREE

THE LADDER

CHAPTER 5

THE EXPLAINER

0^{33} The morning after

I was assigned to something called Strategic Portfolio Advisor (which I learned was a "product," not a person or even a group) in Jersey City, NJ. We knew that about 50% of the assignments were in the Plainsboro headquarters, 40% in New York City (seemed glamorous) and 10% in Jersey City. I didn't really know where Jersey City was, but I knew it wasn't Plainsboro (odd sigh of relief) and not New York City (sorta bummed as there was a positive stigma to anyone who got those assignments).

About an hour later, my "black car" was approaching the Holland Tunnel. I thought to myself, "Ohhhh, they must have messed up, and I actually got one of these super cool assignments in New York City." As we were starting to approach the tunnel, I saw a sign hanging from one of two red brick towers above the tunnel entrance. It simply said, "If you lived here, you'd be home now." Clever, I thought.

As we got closer to the tunnel, the driver veered off to the right and up a ramp. We weren't going into Manhattan. We were, unbeknownst to me, actually in Jersey City. We made our way down a mile or two along the water to an area called Exchange Place.

Again, this was 1998. There had been very little development yet along the "Gold Coast" of Jersey City. You could easily see New York City across the river for almost the entire drive. That building in Exchange Place would be my office for the next seven years. And one of those red brick towers was indeed where I lived the next four.

It was B'shert.

0[34] The explainer

A few years later, I was chatting with a colleague in a similar-sized cubicle. Like me, she was an assistant vice president. Man, the number of titles that exist in some pockets of corporate American is baffling.

I suppose if I think about it, though, perhaps it's one of the most common forms of lily pads out there (more on lily pads later in its own Carry). I mean, imagine if you told a new hire out of college that maybe, one day, in, like 10,000 to 15,000 days, you'd become CEO. But until then, head down and crush it! The other side of that riverbed would appear to be an ocean away. Corporate titling is a form of lily pads.

So, back to my conversation with the AVP (meantime, my sci-fi geekdom can't ever unsee *Alien versus Predator* when I see the AVP title).

There we were, me and the other AVP, not to be confused with me as a Predator and she as an Alien, just two colleagues climbing up the proverbial corporate ladder. Which I, might add, is not a normal shaped ladder, as there is very little room to stand as you ascend. People pretty much are hanging on for dear life on the top rungs. Usually stomping on the fingers of anyone trying to get to their rung (sorta why Ed prompted me to leap off!).

We were prepping for a prospect meeting. At the time, we

worked in an area of the firm that helped support any of the 15,000+ financial advisors who had a $25 million+ opportunity. Even today, that's a very large client, and back in the 2002 era, that was a ginormous client.

Clients could run the gamut between a wealthy family, a union pension fund, a wonderful not-for-profit foundation, you name it—there was no specific source of wealth required. If you had a large amount of money, you'd make your way to our group.

My team would create a ton of things that mattered to these clients. Most important, we had software within our group that, at the time, was cutting edge. What you could now easily download on your iPhone with one bar of service in the middle of a highway with an 80mph speed limit, was only available to our group within the firm. My colleague drafted the information we'd provide. I, in turn, explained the output she created to the financial advisor, and the financial advisor would then share what I'd said with the client or prospect.

So, we were prepping for the meeting, and it became obvious that she was frustrated. Not at me, but the situation. I was the one flying out to South Dakota the next day (or maybe it was North Dakota. I really can't remember anymore. Not implying they are the same state or even similar. I just know I went to both states randomly back-to-back at some point and can't for the life of me remember which trip was which.) It became clear that the knowledge base of asset allocation (that's what the creator was making) mattered, but it could be learned relatively quickly with a lot of intense exposure over a couple of years. It wasn't a scarce commodity. The relationship I had formed with the financial advisor in the preceding weeks, established trust and credibility for the upcoming prospect meeting, and it was irreplaceable.

Back then I traveled every week. I remember being in one of the Dakotas and waking up the morning of my meeting realizing I had forgotten my electric razor in New Jersey. For most people this would be a non-issue. But not for me. I do have very vivid memories of my dad's face slathered with shaving cream, like a close-cut Santa Beard (probably more like Hanukkah Harry, but the Santa Visual is better.) I mean, it went all the way from his sideburns, across his face, dipping under his nose, then down, past his Adam's Apple. Like a full-on face-and-reverse-turtleneck of shaving cream. That visual is not only etched into my brain, but it was a constant. My dad LOVED a good shave. And rarely went a day or two not shaving.

Now, here I was, in a Dakota, probably 25 years old, a bar-mitzvah (or baker's dozen) number of years away from puberty, and I had NEVER applied the shaving cream turtleneck. I had never even shaved my face with a normal Bic style razor. My dad never taught me. To this day, I have no clue why not. Alas, I found my way to a CVS early in the morning and bought a new electric razor. At nearly 50, I still need to pack a clunky electric razor any time I travel. I still have never shaved without one.

OK, back to the scene. So, there I was, sitting in the AVPs guest chair, prepping for the Dakota meeting. And she was pissed. She didn't explicitly ask to come (not that it would have been my call anyway), but I could tell she was asking herself, "Why on earth was this financial advisor in a 'Dakota' asking HIM to come meet the client and explain all the work that I had created?"

What jumped out at me was simple: My organization cared about and rewarded the explainers, not the creators. And I was an explainer. It didn't matter what the subject was, I was able to distill any topic at that point in life, once I learned it, and make it relevant and relatable to my audience. Unbeknownst to me, that 7:04am call I had gotten in Princeton post my Super Saturday on a Tuesday, positioned me to thrive. My communication skills put me there.

CREATOR VERSUS EXPLAINER

Explaining any creation, and why it matters, is crucial to the success of any invention, product enhancement, service offering and other things you're selling. If you are a creator, learn how to explain. Contextualize the thing that's been created in a way that it matters to the person you're talking about. Eliminate jargon. Use the barbecue test. How would you explain that thing to your great aunt over the burgers and buttery corn on the cob? Master the language. Become fluent (not Duolingo). Ultimately, creators are crucial, but without an ability to explain what's been created, your great idea or service may simply go undiscovered and eventually extinct.

What if you're the explainer, not the creator? Find amazing creations to talk about. All the explaining in the world won't save you if what you're selling is meh.

0^{35} The three pillars of a career

What finally hit me: there were three pillars of a career:

1. Skill sets
2. Knowledge bases
3. Relationships

I would argue that, on average, skill sets are the most commoditized and replaceable, but they give you tremendous optionality. Knowledge bases take time to acquire, and if domain expertise is valued in a role or environment, they are potentially worth more than the skill set itself. And relationships are the hardest to form and the hardest to replace. As long as the environment and role you are in support them, they represent the Holy Grail of scarcity and related value.

CAREER PILLARS

Keep lists when it comes to the three pillars of a career: skill sets, knowledge bases and relationships. The lists should include the things you are best at, or where you stand out with unique talents and capabilities. Refresh these lists over time. And actively use them to find new roles and organizations. Typically, relationships are the most valuable part of your career. Authentic ones take a long time to build. Make sure you're in a work/volunteer/environment supportive of building and maintaining them.

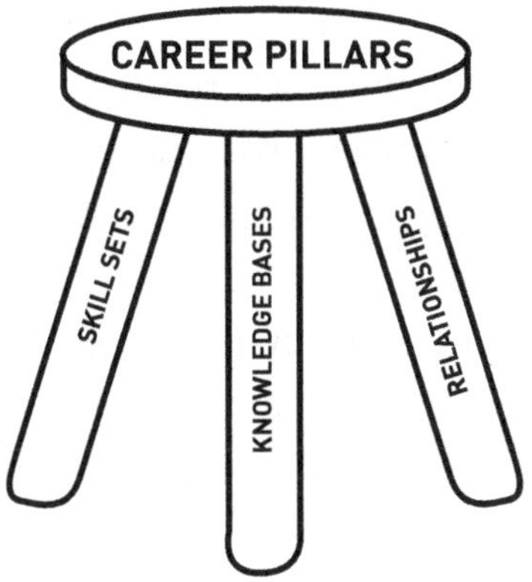

0[36] Three layers deep

So, here I was, 25 years old. I hadn't spent nearly as much time acquiring the knowledge that the creator had, and I didn't know as much as she did, but I had learned enough to be credible and relatable. The utility curve of the excess knowledge at that point didn't matter. I could go three layers deep, likely at least a layer deeper than a prospect would care. So, while she could tunnel a hole below me to the crust of the earth, it didn't matter. The client wouldn't care. I had learned to go deep enough until a depth I knew was sufficient, and pop back out of that hole and deploy the knowledge.

0[37] Reading the room

Success wasn't just about being a great explainer, AKA salesperson. Backing up a month or two, I had gotten a call from the financial advisor in the Dakotas region about a prospect. I had spent hours over multiple conversations with this advisor over the course of the months leading up to it. We got to know one another at a personal level. I taught him about the competition. I explained how I'd explain the asset allocation that the AVP creator was building. I pumped him up with confidence that he had the New York expert flying in to help him close the biggest prospect of his multi-decade career. I believed it. I was sincere.

And…I had been prematurely titled and had gone through puberty a long time ago. I mean, I was 25, so that wasn't surprising—plus, we already discussed my shaving situation.

But what I didn't mention was my voice. It was deep. I mean, older-man deep. So creepily deep that my eighth-grade honors art teacher (zero clue why they even had honors art and how I got into the class) used to say, when I'd answer a question, with her back turned to me on purpose as if she was closing her eyes: "Is there a man in the room?" Wow, that would NOT fly these days. But back then it surely did and was sorta funny.

Even post-chanting my Haftorah at my Bar Mitzvah (for those that have never been to one, it takes place during this religious ceremony at a synagogue when mostly pre-pubescent boys and girls are told they are now men and women after singing/chanting a very long story in Hebrew) – my friends all were like "Yo Adrian" as a tribute to my Rocky-like deep voice – at the age of 13.

So, leading up to the meeting, my deep voice had been saying all of the things the advisor needed to hear and learn for months. I was an expert in his mind's eye. But I was not whom he was expecting to see through his actual eyes, when I met him two hours before the meeting for the first time.

I saw it in his face. Who is this kid? THIS is my New York expert I've been telling my prospect about for months? He couldn't rationalize in his brain that this voice on the other end of the phone had been me. He envisioned a man with greyish hair and some wrinkles. Not my full head of brown hair and electric-shaved, smooth, rosy skin. Even to this day at nearly 50, I'm called "baby face" by colleagues and friends. I likely looked like a high school kid shadowing his dad as an intern. This must be a joke.

All of that ran through my brain in about 2-3 seconds when I saw his blood-drained face. I extended my hand to shake his, which was attached to an arm, that was attached to a body, that supported a head that encased a set of eyes, that were still looking past me, scouring the room for my dad. "Will the real Adam Katz, please stand up. Please stand up!"

Then we finally sat down and talked. I spoke in the same voice. Using the same words. With the same confidence. Only it was coming out of a vessel he didn't expect.

By the end of the one-hour prep session, the blood returned to his face and his shoulders puffed back up to at least the level of those bad women's blazers from the eighties, with football player shoulder pads. He was ready. He was confident.

And that was a very important lesson. Going forward, I would never fly in on the day of a meeting, or as in that case, late the night before. I would always arrive the day before and grab dinner with the advisor. I'd let them absorb the shock of my youthful appearance and get it out of their system. We'd eat. We'd talk. We'd restore the mojo. They'd sleep on it and wake up the next day invigorated that the expert was there to help them win. And we did win, a lot.

THE UNDERDOG CONCEPT

The smaller soccer player. The younger looking team member. Somone from Smalltown, USA. People naturally have attributes that immediately trigger doubt in others. They oddly expect "less" from this person. You can artificially create these types of attributes as well. Be mindful of yours and use them. If you are bucketed incorrectly, your starting position is an advantage. Underdogs are graded on a curve. If an underdog is "good," they immediately are considered "great." And if they are "great", they are considered the "best." Be mindful of this concept and use it with purpose.

0^{38} Staying out of elevator shafts

Over the next few years, I must have traveled with my electric razor at least once a week. The map with the pins was getting full across all 50 states (hence the melding of the Dakotas). I probably did over 100 meetings with everyone ranging from an entrepreneur who sold a company for $40 million to the trustees of a $500 million endowment and the head of a $300 million union.

I learned to find the balance between humility and confidence, and the difference between confidence and arrogance. I spoke to people about what they cared about. If it was a nonprofit, I explained that this asset allocation was going to help them achieve their spending needs, so that they could fund all the grants they wanted and have the maximum impact on their mission…with the least amount of stress along the way. I wasn't going 17 levels deep like the AVP creator wanted to. The clients wouldn't have cared. I would have lost them on the way down the subterranean elevator shaft. I was explaining to them why the topics we were discussing mattered to them. Again, I was fortunately in an environment that highly valued a communication skillset. At that point I had acquired ample knowledge to accompany the skill. I was off to the races.

Meanwhile, what was I doing? I was massively deploying my communication skillset and *explaining*. I was acquiring unique knowledge not only about asset allocation but also what and how to speak to very large clients of varying sources of wealth.

When I think about it, I had more meetings with large prospects than ANY single advisor at the firm. Most, even the BEST advisors at my firm, would hope to have 5-10 of these in any one year. Maybe. I had 20-30 per year for a few years. I had more data points and first-hand experience "pitching" this asset level client than anyone there. And I was 28 years old.

PATTERN RECOGNITION

Look in that rear view mirror often. It's there for a reason. While it's always important to look ahead and consider what comes next, studying what happened in the past will help you see patterns. The more you specialize in something, the more repetitions you'll experience. Eventually commonalities and patterns will emerge. Recognize when they are forming and what they can help you consider in that next opportunity or interaction. Use these observations with care. Absent that, your behavior will look presumptuous, not anticipatory.

0[39] The Katz Kurve

These experiences helped shape an entire career framework I affectionately refer to as the Katz Kurve. I'm not really sure why I named it after myself, which I've avoided in every other framework.

Unintentionally, I had become an expert in the ultra-high-net-worth and institutional client base AND their investment needs. And lastly, and arguably most importantly, I had become the go-to resource across the country. Top advisors knew me. Branch managers in local offices knew me. The head of the sales force knew me. I had built a reputation and credibility. I had formed genuine relationships. The Katz Kurve had a steep angle.

But I was making relatively little money. And hence the second curve of the two-part Katz Kurve was formed. Before we get into the duality of the Kurves, here is a quick visual. For go-forward nomenclature, we'll simply refer to one Kurve as the Pillars Kurve (as in the three career pillars: skill sets, knowledge bases, and relationships) and the Accolades Kurve (think of it as money, titles, stuff like that).

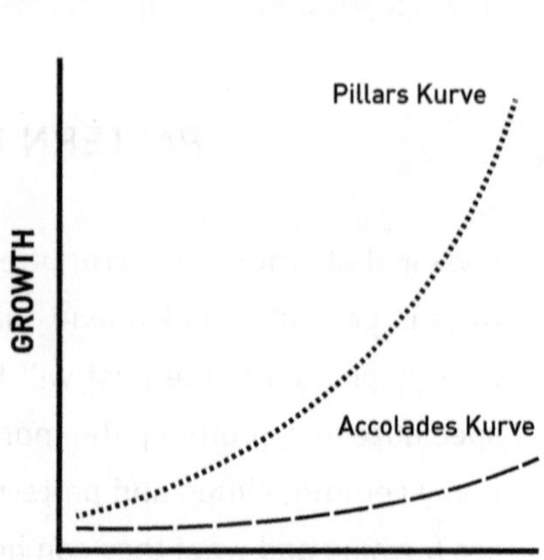

So, around that time, I started to get a bit confused. I felt successful. I was getting amazing validation. I had a ton of responsibility. But I wasn't making that much money and hadn't seen much income growth over those same several years. I mean, frequent flyer miles are cool in your twenties, but they weren't income. I hadn't really been focusing on it at that point so it didn't matter to me so much, but as we all know, two things can be true at the same time. I was getting fucked.

That said, I could fix it if I intentionally changed the angle of the Pillars Kurve and deployed all that I had acquired (the skill sets, knowledge bases and relationships) into an environment that might value it much more highly.

Think about the above graphic progressing like this:

By deploying your Pillars Kurve assets in the right environment, you can monetize them (versus acquiring more) and recognize a big acceleration in your Accolades Kurve.

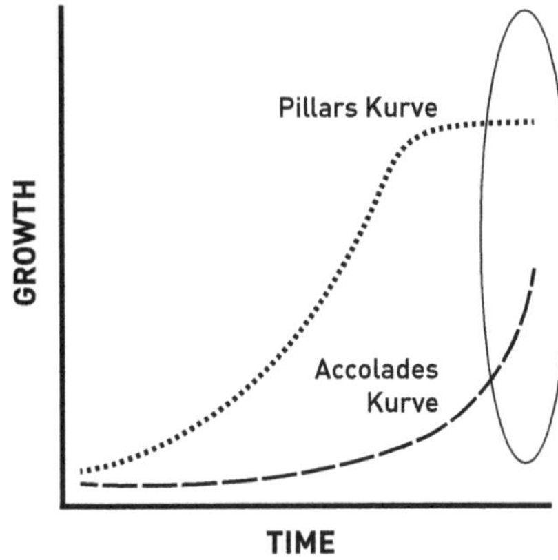

KATZ KURVE

Careers are typically defined by accolades. Things like promotions and titles, compensation, equity grants etc. Think of those as lagging indicators, the *results,* not the *goals* themselves. Focus on your three career pillars. Accumulate those as you can control that curve. These will accelerate faster than your "career." Be mindful of which of the pillars you are acquiring and make sure to deploy them and get rewarded. Recognize during the deployment phase, you will see the career accolades more visibly. Interestingly, you'll likely notice that the acquisition of new skills, knowledge bases and relationships may slow during these periods – and that the Pillars Kurve flattens. That's OK. Give yourself grace. Be mindful of this dynamic as it likely will repeat over and over again in life, with ever-increasingly shorter cycles.

PART FOUR

MEANS

CHAPTER 6

ANY GIVEN TUESDAY

0^{40} Selective denominators

I love how people calibrate things based on denominators that make them feel better, worse, more dramatic, etc. Early in my career as a wealth advisor, a partner of mine said a new prospect was going to send us a "quarter million dollars," as the barely-about-to-be client put it. Dude. It's $250,000. I mean, that's not no money, but stop dressing it up as a close cousin to $1,000,000. Funny.

My favorite is baby and toddler calibration. *My son is 9 weeks old. My twins are 28 weeks old. My nephew is 13 months old.* It's around 24 months when you just start saying, "My kid is two." Time, as you're learning, the calibration of it, is one of my favorite topics. I still can't get over how we thought we'd have flying cars (with an eerily quiet jet-like retrofitted engine) by 2015. Zemeckis had us going.

YOUR OWN TIME MACHINE

A minute is a minute. A day is a day. A month is a month. A year is a year. But. And that's a big "but." The way in which you look at those units of time can change your perspective dramatically.

Here's my easiest example: Is the next year 100% of YOUR time, or 5% of the next 20 years? If you live in the 100% camp, most things this upcoming year will feel urgent. You've got to pack them in immediately before "time runs out." However, if you hop in a time machine 20 years ahead, and look back, this next year is only 5% of the next 20. You will inherently be more patient. Things will feel like they are moving more slowly. And you'll likely make decisions that optimize for longer term happiness and alignment.

1 MONTH

January 2026						
1	2	3	4	5	6	7
8	9	10	11	12	13	14
15	16	17	18	19	20	21
22	23	24	25	26	27	28
29	30	31				

5 YEARS = 60 MONTHS

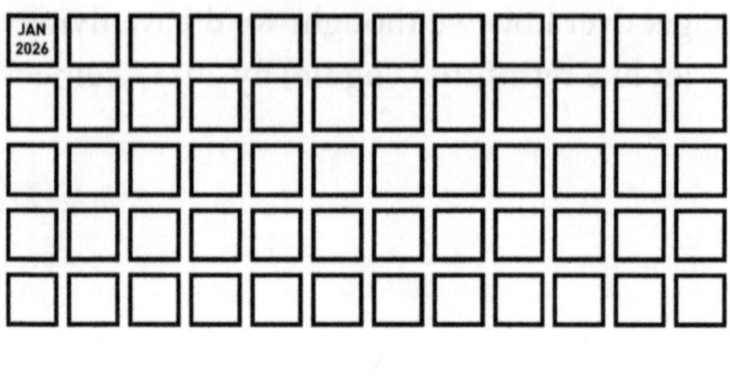

0[41] First class

So, as I began to work with ultra-high-net-worth clients, I found that as you start to accumulate some wealth or feel like you're on the precipice of a step-function wealth creation event, your brain can't help but daydream about what life could look like. There's the experiential shit. Vacations. How you fly perhaps (Holy shit! Flying first class *might* be the most polarizing topic I've ever discussed with people). The opportunity to take that African safari. Help out your parents, or a nephew. Donate to a local organization you are passionate about. Or maybe. Just maybe. Buy stuff. Nice stuff. Jewelry. Watches. Handbags. Cars. You name it. Things. Possessions. Mother-fucking-materialistic-shit.

Oddly, people almost shun buying things when they have money. It's a weird badge of "Oh, I don't need anything like that. I don't care about blah, blah, blah."

Then who the fuck is buying all these luxury goods?!

And that, alas, is what I wanna dive into. We'll tackle this from a few angles, but the main thing I coach my clients on, post a step-function liquidity event, is to *take it out for a spin*.

I use this phrase in a few ways, but for now we'll focus on trying things. Lots of different things. See where you find utility. See where you feel wasteful.

Buy a nice car. Or at least drive a bunch of them. There is a certain level of car that is simply *better*. It's quieter. It's got better pickup for merging onto a highway. It likely has a sick sound system. Probably looks nicer if you're into that. Doesn't need to be a Ferrari or Bentley but go check them out. That's the most literal version of "taking it out for a spin."

Try donating to a charity you connect with, in a meaningful way. Put an extra zero or two onto what you'd usually give. Speak with the executive director and ask about the *impact* of your dollars.

Pay for a family vacation with your folks and siblings and nieces and nephews. Get a suite at the local sports stadium for a game on *any given Sunday* 😊.

Try. Shit. Out.

And then… figure out what your jam is.

But here is where things get interesting. What if you could buy that watch? That handbag. That Ferrari. On any given Tuesday? Like, you have a break in your day, and you can pop over to the mall and spend $30,000 on a watch. Or $10,000 on a purse. Or $1,000 on some cool sneakers. Or $350,000 on a Ferrari. We won't dive into the fact that in many / all of these cases, even if you have the willingness to buy / pay, they may not actually sell you the product based on actual or real inventory levels. It's a maddening dynamic of having wealth and not being able to actually acquire the things you want!

Well, they don't sell Ferraris in the malls. Only the electric car showrooms seem to have replaced some of my old favorite clothing stores. (So weird to see cars where racks of clothing used to be.)

Anyway, you get the point. But here's the rub: once you *can* buy that Ferrari on any given Tuesday and you *don't* have any urge to, you may start to question your pre-wealth daydreaming.

PASSION OR ASPIRATION

If you can go buy that thing you've always coveted on any given Tuesday, but never get around to it, ask yourself why. Presuming you've gotten comfortable with your relationship to money, and you realize the purchase doesn't move the needle via the 3-digit rule or your new units of money, why aren't you buying it? Or planning that trip, concert or game?

You may realize that that things and experiences you bucketed aren't really passions of yours. They are simply things that you had previously coveted when you couldn't afford them. You thought they were passions, but they weren't. They were simply masquerading as such.

If you can now purchase the Ferrari but never make it to the dealership, maybe you no longer want one. This goes for experiences as well. Be active and discerning about what you want in your life. There is nothing bad about dropping them from your priority list.

042 Visible versus invisible wealth

Building on the themes above, one thing that's occurred to me over the last couple of decades, and more acutely the past couple of years, has to do with what people can "see" and what is invisible.

Let's start with the easy stuff. Jewelry. Lululemon leggings.

Watches. Fully portable things. They're visible to EVERYONE who meets you, whether in person or when you post pictures of yourself on social media.

Then we'll get to the next level. Cars. People can see them, but not when you're on vacation and meet someone at a resort or you start chatting with someone on a plane in first class (there it is again!). I mean, you can post a douchey picture of yourself on social media with your fancy car, but it's unlikely a new acquaintance will see it.

And even when you're at home, if you park your car in your garage (not even your driveway) people only see it when you get in and out of it at the mall or local eateries. Or when you hang with your friends. Other people around town may catch a peek when you go to Starbucks or things like that, but your vehicle of choice, despite its wheels, is not nearly as "portable" as your Rolex Daytona, Van Cleef necklace, or Hermès tie.

Ha, ties. Zemeckis got that one wrong, too!

Okay, you see where we're going with this.

Next, let's get to the most typical show of wealth: your house. You can't bring it on vacation with you, either. It's not with you at the grocery store or at Cartier. You can own it with some anonymity in an LLC or something similar and make it pretty hard to search your name and find your home.

So…your home is usually only visible to people you invite over. Or some neighbors that put 2+2 together. And if you have more than one house, the only people who know about the other house(s) are the people you tell or invite.

Now let's get to the other stuff. The complete opposite side of wealth. The giving. Helping your nephew pay for college. Funding mom and dad's retirement and healthcare. Putting an addition on your local church or synagogue. Extensions of my Random Acts of Daily Financial Kindness concept on tipping, which is coming up soon.

It's the stuff no one really knows about. It's the stuff people can't see. And often, it's at magnitudes that make the stuff you can see look tiny. Inconsequential.

And this confuses many people.

0[43] The tip of the iceberg

The proverbial "tip of the iceberg" is a concept that has got a lot of applicability to this whole framing of what people can see regarding your wealth—and how confusing it can be to others.

Now, some may say, instinctively, "Who gives a shit about what other people think?" or "People should mind their own business and not judge." Well, okay, but I would argue most don't truly feel, or more importantly, act that way.

So, let's presume people check each other out.

And there are two of them. Each has a nice car when they pull up to a local eatery. Valet takes them both and anoints them worthy of the coveted "front positions" in the lot for everyone to see. Backed in.

It's funny that restaurants, hotels, and any places that are hospitality-oriented believe that adorning their establishment with fancy cars makes other people want to come in. I have no clue if this is true, but it's a consistent strategy.

Anyway, you are each waiting post-dinner for the valet to drive your car to you about 15 feet away and you're sizing each other up. Let's not go extreme here, but we'll presume you both have $150,000 to $200,000 cars. Nothing exotic. Maybe a Porsche and a higher-end Mercedes model.

Both wives have Chanel bags, some Cartier and Van Cleef adorning their necks and Rolex and Patek's ensnaring their wrists. Maybe Gucci loafers. All of it.

The guy in the Porsche gives the valet a $1 bill. The guy in the Mercedes gives the valet a $20 bill. No one is aware except the valets. The other people waiting for their cars don't know the difference. (Again, more on my tipping philosophy and construct in a little while.)

Those two folks look pretty similar… from what people can *see*.

Then, they both leave. The Porsche driver and his wife pull up to their McMansion in a crappy town that they bought for $1.5 million with an 80% loan-to-value mortgage when rates were in the 2%'s… so to be specific, the Porsche folks' home purchase looked like this:

- 20% down ($300,000 out of pocket)
- $1.2 million mortgage (10-year interest only at 2.5% = $30,000/year or $2,500/month for the mortgage – probably *less* than their Porsche lease payment!!!)

The Mercedes couple drives a little farther to their Class A town. They pull up to their 100-year-old home that they bought for $2 million in cash and then gut-renovated the inside and revamped the entire 1.5-acre property to include a pool, pool house, and a tennis court.

All in, they spent $5 million in cash. No mortgage for now. They might take out one if/when rates come back lower.

So, we haven't scratched the surface, because I'm going to keep going.

To the other folks in the valet line, they look pretty similar. Same stuff on their body. Same type of car.

But the Porsche family had to come up with $300,000 for their home out of pocket. The Mercedes family, $5,000,000. Not even the same stratosphere of wealth.

The Porsche family may make $800,000/year. Very nice living (depending on where you live, maybe less nice). Keep $400,000/year after taxes. So, figure repeating 3s: about $33,333/month. Love shit like that. Didn't even do that one on purpose.

Can that couple "afford" a Porsche lease for $2,000/month? Sure. Mortgage on the McMansion for $2,500/month? Sure. Buying the "stuff" that everyone on the valet line can see? Easy.

And this is why money is very confusing.

But let's keep going.

What I didn't mention is that the couples know each other. They're friends. Their kids go to the same private school for $50,000/year. Again, it's like $4,200/month.

The Porsche couple can "afford" it. Mercedes couple's 3-digit rule makes that unit of money indiscernible.

But again, at the school events, they both show up in the parking lot with "similar" cars. They have a lot of the same belongings. They have been to each other's houses. Done some Zillowing. This gives some directionality to the Mercedes family's wealth, but not really.

Then we keep going.

Winter break time. The Mercedes family flies first class to their vacation destination. The resort they are going to costs $50,000 for the week. All-in cost, probably $70,000.

The Porsche family also goes on vacation. Coach flights. Points used. Staying at a different type of resort, $10,000 for the week. Different type of vacation.

Unless you are posting all of this on social media, that $60,000 difference is invisible.

And this is nothing. The Mercedes family donates $100,000/year to charities. The Porsche family, $3,000/year. The Mercedes family has $20 million in their brokerage accounts. The Porsche family has $1 million.

People never know what is beneath the surface. You only know what people want you to see.

In the scheme of material wealth, the shoes, the bags, the watches, even the cars (via leases) tell you very little. Beneath the surface, is an invisible iceberg used for private experiences, supporting family and friends and maybe, charity.

Or perhaps there is nothing. A popsicle stick bobbing beneath the surface. Bare. Naked. Whittled down to its fleshy, soggy, tooth-mark laden wood. As the popsicle bobs at the surface for everyone to see.

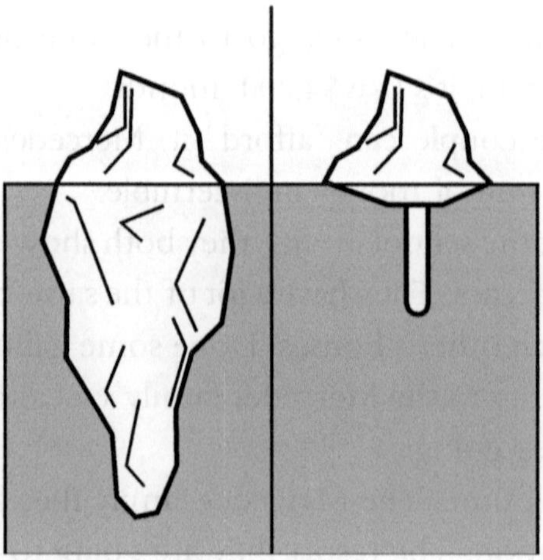

ICEBERG OR POPSICLE STICK?

What you know about many people's wealth in only what they show you. Most of that is on their body, the car they drive, the house they live in, the vacation they show on Instagram. But you never know what lies beneath the surface: Do they own these things? Rent them? What does the rest of their life look like? Usually, the most visible forms of wealth don't cost that much in the scheme of real money. Is there anything beneath the tip of the iceberg? What you see tells you very little.

0[44] Raising kids in a Zillow world

When most of us grew up, we knew nothing about how much our parents spent, nor how much they helped other people via general familial/friend financial support or actual charity and donations. There was perfect symmetry in both columns of this imaginary ledger. We knew shit about shit.

Well, the information age has blown that construct into a gazillion pieces and created a massively lopsided, asymmetric accounting statement.

Kids can look up how much everything costs. And at a way earlier age than you think. They look up what houses cost. What cars cost. Vacations. Jewelry etc. So, regardless of what you tell them, they know what you are spending. You have no choice. Now, they of course have no clue what percentage of your income or balance sheet that represents, but it certainly matters in absolute dollars. The numerator absent the denominator is still relatable dollars to a kid. So. What Dana and I decided to do, is tell our kids exactly what we donate – and more importantly "why" we choose to do it. My kids are intimate with my tipping construct and why we leave restaurants quickly after I sign or tap given the Random Acts of Daily Financial Kindness philosophy (I promise, we're almost there on this one!). In an uncontrollably asymmetric financial information world, we've been extremely intentional and deliberate by making both sides of the Katz Family Financial Ledger harmonious, like the olden days.

Be mindful of this. This one is not intuitive. But at this point it is fact. You have no choice but to even the scales by talking to your kids, friends and family about all the things that matter to you and ways you are using your financial wealth for others, not just yourselves. And if you're not helping others at a level that makes the ledger look balanced (subjective word here), get the fuck going. Being visible and vocal about these efforts can evoke strong emotions in others, across the spectrum below – motivating people to expand their charitable efforts and generosity.

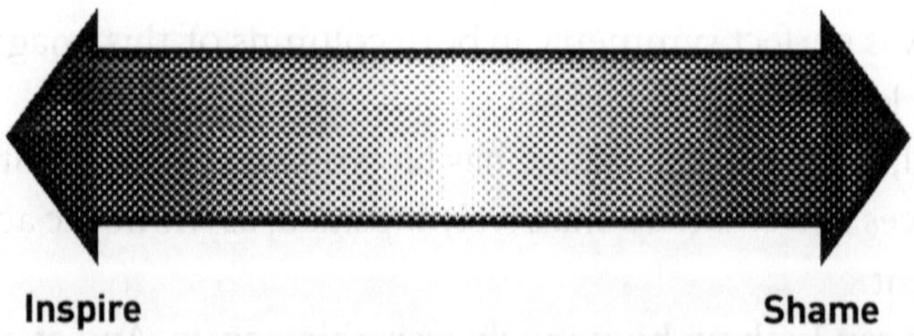

PART FIVE

TIME MACHINE

CHAPTER 7

THE GHYME

0^{45} "Back in the day"

I used to start sentences with "Back in the day..." What was I doing? I was 32. That day was "the day." But I had already started speaking as if life had passed me by. No matter what successes you're racking up in your career, you still can't escape one reality: You're a human being, living in a physical body. If you don't take care of it, you won't be able to enjoy all of the rewards in your life for very long.

My son was around two years old at the time. And I'd get winded chasing him around during silly gym classes.

My waist? 43 inches. Not that I bought 43" jeans — who does that? I bought 36" stretch jeans and shoved them under my belly. One day at the GHYME (Holy shit, Homer Simpson, your walkabout at night when you saw the neon sparkling in the GYM and asked, "What's a GHYME?" will forever stay etched in my brain and now in the consciousness of you folks reading it, too), the trainer whipped out the tape measure: 43" belly. I was like "Ummm" in my own Homer Simpson vernacular. Even worse, my chest was similar. While I didn't look exactly like Homer, this body type can best be described as SpongeBob SquarePants torso.

And while I love geometry (i.e., all squares are rectangles, but

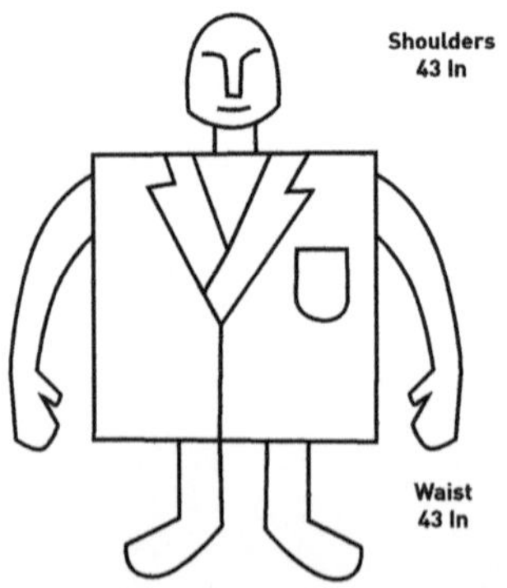

not all rectangles are squares), this body wasn't the shape I wanted.

So, I started going to the GHYME. That was a good addition to my sedentary lifestyle at the ripe old age of 32, but wasn't going to move the needle alone. A friend said something simple: "There are 3,500 calories in a pound." (To be candid, I'm Googling this right now to make sure it's accurate. Does it make me look old to say that these days? Am I just supposed to "ask" Google or Siri? Let's try that! "Hey Siri, how many calories are in a pound?" In 1958, it was 3,500 calories, per some scientist. Wow, that was cool. So yes, 3,500 calories is a pound.) And then it dawned on me. It was just one big math equation. And if we truly add up our daily food intake, it's always a lot more than we think.

The real issue is the microtransactions in each distinct interaction with your food. Whether it be breakfast time, snack time, coffee break time, snack time, dinner time, snack time, after-GYHME time, before-GHYME time, at-the-movie-theater-time, at-the-airport-time, at your kid's five-year-old birthday party time, at-the-Super Bowl-party-time, at your-birthday-dinner time, at Thanksgiving … there is ALWAYS a special time for eating. And by compartmentalizing and rationalizing within each of those microtransactions with food, we gravitate to two things:

1. Eventicizing: Each meal is its own self-contained event to be celebrated.
2. Numerators and Denominators: This leads to the "Just one more" mindset versus considering what else we ate at THAT meal.

0^{46} Pizza

As you might have guessed, my tendency to brainstorm and see patterns in the mundane came into play with weight loss. The real issue was all these microtransactions have a cumulative and long-lasting impact. They happen so slowly, it's easy to justify each decision and claim ignorance of any impact it may have over the next month, year, or decade. Our brains simply can't process information that way. We like instant gratification. "Just one more" is soooooo easy.

So, I went in the other direction and started saying "just one less." What if I started tracking all the things I WANTED to eat at every kid's birthday party, or on a Saturday night with friends, or at the Super Bowl party, or at the colleague's birthday lunch at work, or at a bris for a friend's newborn son? When you start thinking about it, you can find a "meal event" almost every day of the week and rationalize that they are ALL special.

And then, within the microtransaction, it's just "one more brownie, they're soooo good." Or, I'll just have two more shots with my buddies, because they got a new job. Or it's 11 a.m. on a Tuesday and I'm at my friend's kid's bris and I've already had breakfast and have a lunch meeting, but man, I haven't had a bagel and lox with cream cheese in sooo long (well, since my other friend's kid's Bar Mitzvah three weeks ago) and I "deserve" it.

Oh man, there is a lot of deserving...justifying. Meals become "events," not simply sustenance. Now I'm not saying we shouldn't celebrate food. I'm going somewhere much more interesting. I love food. But I believe the fundamental issue is our microtransactions with food during specific "event meals."

Our elation, and the visible utility from indulging in the moment ("It's an event') AND that we can't "see" the impact of the extra brownie, pizza slice, beer, bagel for many weeks/months/years is the very paradigm I've turned on its head.

JUST ONE LESS

The reason people often treat themselves to "just one more" is because they eventicize the situation and /or they compartmentalize things into a microtransaction. Don't. Use your mental time machine and fast forward a few hours or days. Zero chance you'll be upset you didn't have that extra donut or extra beer. In the moment, it might feel like it'll bring you real joy and enhance the experience. But it simply doesn't matter. Make a list of all the things you skipped or didn't do. You'll be shocked at what the summation of your "just one less" list looks like in a week.

0^{47} Birthday parties

For any of you that have small kids, or who were small kids... ya know, all of us. One of the hallmarks of that era of life is pizza parties. Besides my daughter, I've never met anyone who doesn't like pizza. How she doesn't like pizza is a mystery. I mean, it's the perfect food. So easy to eat. Delicious hot or cold, even if it's relatively shitty pizza. Contrasting this with pretty shitty Chinese food. Most people ball that crunchy chicken right up and spit it anywhere that's not their mouth.

But everyone loves pizza, except my daughter. She takes off the cheese (the best part) and then eats soggy bread with sauce. Gross. She also doesn't like cake, not normal cake. She sorta likes cupcakes and loves a good Carvel ice cream cake with the black crunchies.

So, getting back to the other 99.99%. Pizza parties. They're just an inevitable part of birthday parties for multiple years, and not just your own kids'. I mean, ALL of the kids' birthday parties you are forced to go to for a good five to seven years. Figure there are 20–30 kids in their school class. We aren't in click world yet, and everyone gets invited to EVERY party. Maybe you even throw in a sports team, or a religious school, and you easily have 40–50 birthday kids' parties you go to every year.

They're at little gym places, like the one where I was getting winded running around after my son. Pottery places. Bowling lanes. Regardless, the meal is always the same: pizza. It's easy (everyone besides my daughter likes it). It's relatively cheap. It's a great leftover for the hosting family when an overzealous parent inevitably orders too much.

But it's A LOT of pizza. Sure, you can say "No, thanks." Or see if they ordered some sad, wilted salad. But you're gonna be eating some pizza, maybe two slices every time. Oh, I didn't even mention all the times you just go to some friends' houses for pizza… another dozen times a year. Maybe two dozen.

So, I did the math that people don't like. It told me that on average, I was easily consuming 150–200 slices of pizza a year. But what if I NEVER ATE AN END CRUST AGAIN?

Just one less, I told myself. Each microtransaction has gotta add up. Each party, each slice. Would I miss it? Did it matter that much?

I was able to do the visual. I looked at that party table with the Dora the Explorer plastic tablecloth and envisioned 200 crusts that one year that I DIDN'T EAT. All of those half-moons of unnecessary dough. At each party, it seemed like a non-event to eat it. It was "only *one more*" each time I had two slices. That visual finally made it click.

If I could envision the cumulative impact of the small change of "just one less," I could fast-forward a year and see all the empty carbohydrates and calories I wouldn't eat that year. And when I combined it with my newfound knowledge that 3,500 calories equal a pound, I did the math. The guesstimate was that it's about 75 calories a crust, especially these super large doughy slices that tend to be the destination of choice in the NJ suburbs. So, 75 calories × 200 slices = 15,000 calories or approximately 4.28 lbs.

Now, that number doesn't get that many people excited. It's WAY more thrilling to eat that delicious crust EVERY time than to think about losing 0.02% of a pound every time you don't. It's the built-in handle. It's MEANT to be eaten. It's not a piece of plastic or like an ice cream cone paper holder. It's PART of the meal. What am I doing discarding it?

The impact each time is infinitesimal. And this is the trap. "But this is just the pizza crust." Once you start applying this to a few more things (not EVERYthing, but a few more things) it can easily add up to 15–20 pounds in a year. I imagine for most people looking to lose weight this would be a major success, over a year, to lose that weight healthily, habitually, in a non-fad-diety way.

But it's hard to picture the outcome because of micro-observations and non-correlated and random outcomes over short periods. If I can tell you on January 1 that you get one of my time machines and can see the scale on December 31, BUT that you don't get to look at it in between, a lot more people would get there. But "just one more" crushes "just one less" because of our ability to monitor things in too-real time. And when we don't see any correlation to that daily activity that should, eventually matter in weeks/months, we regress.

There are SO many things that can derail long-termism as it relates to the cumulative impact of these small changes. The scale is our enemy. Connected devices can be another enemy. Our random digestive cycles are enemies.

0[48] The perfect day

You get up. You go for a walk. Empty belly, baby, just like the caveman or cavewoman. Out on a hunt, nothing to eat yet. You come back, have some berries, and maybe some Greek yogurt. Good to go! Lunchtime, some grilled chicken and some broccoli. Handful of nuts at 3 p.m., or 5:30 p.m., a nice 20-minute Peloton HIIT ride. Time for some salmon and sweet potatoes. Handful of pistachios for a little dessert by 7 p.m.

And that's it! You did it. All the things you were supposed to. You moved. You didn't overeat. You didn't have "just one more;" instead you had "just one less" at every interaction with your food. Each meal wasn't an "event" you needed to celebrate.

You didn't eat that leftover chocolate chip pancake from the weekend next to your blueberries in the fridge. You skipped over the leftover pizza box and breadsticks the kids ordered from Domino's. You moved the salt and vinegar baked potato chips in the pantry to get to the pistachios. And you definitely didn't have any of the amazing cupcakes your son baked post-dinner. And you wake up the next day, hop on the scale, and you're UP a half a pound from the day before.

We don't see those results of "just one less" for weeks or months. But on a minute-by-minute basis, we can FEEL and TASTE the joy of microtransactions with food. We can justify them. We can rationalize them. And when we do everything "perfectly" and don't see instant gratification, it's easy to decide it doesn't really matter anyway. It's not gonna work. Fuck this. But those words won't help you lose 15 or 20 pounds. "Just one less" will.

0^{49} From fat to fit

As I said early on, time machines exist. I could envision the scale in 365 days. I didn't know what it would say, but I knew it was a big math equation. By thinking that way, I lost 11" around my waist and 40 pounds in the next year. I did it slowly. I did it patiently. And I did it understanding it was all about "just one less."

I didn't feel deprived. I felt in control. I felt empowered. And my sentences started with words like "Today," "Yesterday," or "Tomorrow" ... never "Back in the Day."

0^{50} Pounds and investment returns

Which brings us back to the zeros in your life...and making them count. What if, on January 1, I asked, "How would you feel if your portfolio was up 15–20% this year?" Most people, besides Jim Simons, would be on board.

Sidebar. I obviously would never say or imply a return like this. It's not realistic. But I wanted to mirror the weight-loss concept from a magnitude perspective for simplicity. And uncomfortably for anyone reading this book, it likely doesn't really matter what your portfolio grows at, unless you are married to some terminal value of your wealth at death. I'll say that again. It doesn't really matter for any practical reason. Remember, the only competition for memory making (experiences, giving, stuff) is some optimization for the biggest denominator at death. I can't recall anyone I've met really subscribing to that goal (or if so, it's a massive minority view and not someone I'd work with). Having eight-, nine- or 10-figure wealth early on pretty much means that as that utility curve for consumption flattens, you likely can't outspend even moderate portfolio growth of 5-7%/year. I'm not having an inflation discussion for those of you trying to butt in regarding real versus nominal growth. Let's talk about a more relevant aspect of "real." You'll still buy all the stuff you want and go on all your vacations, no matter what they cost.

So, back to your portfolio that you can only remember two to three digits from the left anyway. What if I told you that you couldn't look at your portfolio EVER for the whole year. No alerts on your Apple Watch. No Yahoo Finance perusing. Just close your eyes and live your life.

There are strong parallels between losing weight over a year and investment performance of a portfolio over a similar time period. For both frameworks, technology and access to information derail us. They allow "just one more" or super near-term validation and dopamine hits to overshadow the cumulative impact of small changes over time. We know this to be true intuitively, but we have too many ways to interact with data that can take us off track.

At the risk of saying "Back in the day" one more time, 25 to 30 years ago, before the internet was really a thing, people would mostly check their "stocks" 30 to 40 times a year. Still way too much, but that was mostly observations. It was likely done as a perusal with no real math. It was simply taking the physical paper on a Sunday and looking through the stock section for the week in an alphabetical manner.

Now, the irony is back then, it was literally likely a list. Not a portfolio even. You probably didn't even know exactly how much of each stock you had. So, it wasn't really telling much about magnitude but rather directionality. Today, you can see this every second of the day.

How is this helpful? You lost $316,435 today. You can feel that. You can relate it to your everyday life. It's the new pool you wanted to put in. Four years of tuition to college for one of your kids. A blowout vacation with friends on a private plane to a yacht for the week. And you just LOST it today.

But micro-observations of micro transactions and micro timeframes can bedevil us. They misalign us with long-term thinking because they give us dopamine hits on a day-to-day basis. We all KNOW the chart I'm going to show you is true, but we interact with it on a minute-by-minute basis, even though our goals for growing our portfolio or changing our silhouette to a V from a square can take years.

CUMULATIVE IMPACT OF SMALL CHANGE

Related to the "Just one less" framework, it's difficult for the human brain to process the cumulative returns of anything. Whether it be weight loss. Muscle building. Investment returns. Language skills. None of the actions we take in these areas ever feels like real progress. That's why it's important to use that mental time machine. If you eliminate milk from every cup of coffee you drink for 365 days, that change will make a difference. But on a daily or hourly basis, it's easy to say, "Who cares? It doesn't matter." You might think that doing 50 push-ups a day is insignificant. But doing 15,000+ in a year will surely make your arms and chest noticeably stronger and toned. Play around with time. Know these small changes have big impact. Be patient. Rewire your brain.

PART SIX

FREEDOM

CHAPTER 8

LEARNING TO LEAP

0[51] When is your next vacation?

I was talking to a woman I met in my early months at Merrill. Figure she was about 40—almost 10 years younger than I am now, but 18 years my senior at the time. She was a director. Way more important than a senior specialist. Also, a full high-schooler's lifetime ahead of me on the calendar.

I was in a glorified cubicle. Mine had a visitor seat, though. One where the visitor could stare at another unused stack of business cards, resting in one of those tilted holders. (Does anyone actually use business cards anymore?)

Anyway, so there I am, standing up in my relatively ginormous cubicle, barely seeing over the wall, and talking to my colleague. She was in an office. She had a view. Not a corner view, but the kind that, if you got up close to the window and looked sideways, you could see the river and NYC. She had sunlight. There was a pecking order.

I looked up to her. Well, technically, during this interaction, I was oddly looking down at her, as I peered over my cubicle wall that my 5'9" tippy-toed head barely cleared—and there she was across the "hallway / walkway," in her office, seated behind her desk (which had two visitor seats), and we were chatting. About nothing in particular. Small talk, when that existed in the pre-pandemic office culture.

And I offhandedly, and with zero agenda, said, "When's your next vacation?"

Here I was, the cubicle-by-day, 685-foot-by-night dweller asking the office-by-day, suburban-palace-by-night dweller what vacation she was going on that I could join vicariously.

And her answer was, "I don't have one planned."

Sorta sad, sorta weird, I thought. So, I simply said, "Well, you should plan one."

I didn't explain it as articulately then, but it created a framework I describe as lily pads.

0^{52} Frogger's lily pads

Take a calendar year. Those prechosen 365.24 days mostly have little to do with our lives, but as humans, we need to organize ourselves around an arbitrary calendar year. I know, the calendar has a lot to do with science, etc., but just indulge me.

So, you sit there on January 1. And just think about the year visually. Pretend that December 31 is the other side of the river. You can agree that it is pretty much invisible. It is a LONG way away. You can't SEE it, and there is zero chance you could jump to the other side (even if you had my crazy high school jumping abilities). I found that depressing. But fixable.

So, when I heard that my colleague had no vacations planned, that the other side of the river was far away, I realized that simply having a vacation on the calendar would provide massive utility and joy. Because that event was soonish. Maybe six weeks away. Maybe eight weeks away. But that vacation was visible.

Back to the river: that vacation was a lily pad you could not only see but jump to. So, I continued to encourage people to have one. Its mere existence helps you see it. And the fact that you can jump to it provides a near-term dopamine hit.

The trick is to then plan the next vacation. It doesn't need to be fancy. It doesn't need to be long. It just needs to be visible from the first lily pad and jumpable.

Suddenly, the end-to-end riverbed leap is irrelevant. You have converted what was essentially one long slog into micro chapters of the year, always giving yourself something to not only look forward to (which has utility on its own), but to also experience.

Think about how fast Frogger from the classic video game would get across that river with a sea of lily pads.

LILY PADS

Think of markers on the side of a highway, stepping stones in a backyard. We need natural breaks in our lives. Create them. Give yourself lily pads to get across the river or lake of life. Vacations. Hangouts with friends and family.

Be intentional about planning things. Don't let 4-6 weeks go by without doing something different and special. Having it on your schedule provides joy on its own. It's visible. It's soonish. It's reachable. Being able to see it in a reasonable time frame (weeks, not months) is crucial. I always ask people, "When and where is your next vacation?" Have an answer.

0[53] Lifelines

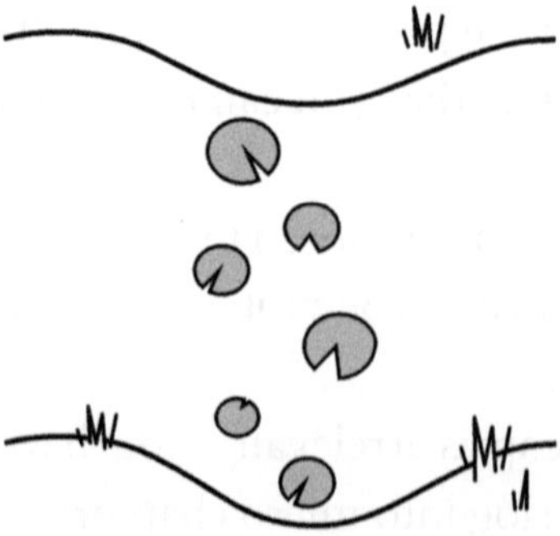

Lily pads are quite literally a frog's lifeline. This isn't Regis Philbin's three lifelines, but these seemingly floating, oversized leaves on the surface of a river or a lake are what allow a frog to stay above the water and out of the way of predators roaming beneath the surface. They allow the frog to get from one side of the river to the other with certainty and safety.

Lily pads are rest stops. The frog can see them. They are amazing jumpers, but this ability is barely needed given how close the lily pads cluster together.

Interestingly, beneath the surface of a lily pad, there is a whole network of veins, tubes, and anatomy. Not pretty like the visible pads, but intricate and purposeful. A pretty cool yin/yang in everyday nature.

A frog can launch itself above the river or lake to chart out a skipping course across a sea of lily pads, as if it has its own drone camera. Frogs can somehow instinctively see a pattern and begin jumping with abandon. With purpose, hope and intentionality. No fear.

0[54] Dangers of the Lily Mismatch

We talked about lilies in the context of a calendar year…and vacations. Being able to jump on the lily on its own provides joy, and even being able to see it brings the anticipation of it. That anticipation itself is its own form of pleasure. It's a wonderful cycle.

But when there's a mismatch of lilies in a relationship, things can go awry. Many years ago, I remember my mom asking me about something. Maybe it was a holiday gathering. I don't remember the exact circumstance. I remember feeling annoyed.

That was because I had "so many other things to think about before that, Mom, that I can't possibly focus on that yet." What I really meant was: "This event you're asking me about in three weeks is a lily pad I can barely see right now and definitely cannot jump to yet (even with my oddly springy legs)."

I'll focus on the lily she wants me to see once I make my way through the seven lily pads that are closer and jumpable. She wasn't trying to be annoying or asking me to skip over other lilies. She just had no other lily pads in front of her, other than the family holiday party three weeks away.

Which brings us to the Lily Mismatch. In relationships, if one person has many lily pads and the other has only a few, even a week can look really different.

Let's say it's Sunday night. A husband asks his wife about Wednesday's soccer game and Friday's college friend get-together. That's it. Those are his two lily pads.

But his wife is a CEO. She travels. She runs meetings. She speaks at conferences. She has two flights that week. Forty-seven meetings. She has 27 lily pads between Sunday and Wednesday night, and another 20 between that and Friday.

That's the Lily Mismatch.

It's solvable with intentionality. Some lily pads are workouts. Some are friend catchups. Some are meetings. Some are volunteering. The point is: if one partner has a few, and the other has dozens, the week can feel wildly out of sync. But if you become aware of the mismatch and weigh the lily pads differently, you can align much more meaningfully in all types of relationships.

THE LILY MISMATCH

Beware the Lily Mismatch. This most often occurs in personal relationships. One spouse has three things going on that week. The other 26. I'm not saying you will be able to sync up your commitments perfectly but be mindful of others' lily pads and how you align in frequency and magnitude. Stay in tune with what the people in your circle have going on in their lives. A mismatch that gets exaggerated and goes unaddressed can cause huge strife in personal relationships.

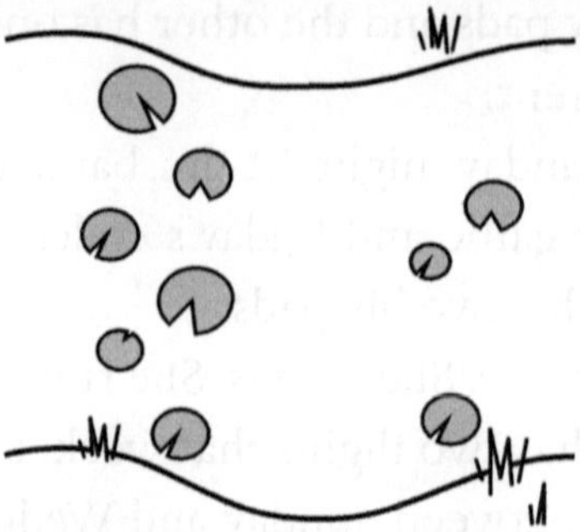

0[55] Traditions are strange

Speaking of milestones, can we discuss those cultural things that, for those not involved in the culture, I think are super strange? How about a bris? For those unfamiliar, it's the ceremony at a Jewish boy's ripe old age of eight days old, where a bunch of friends and family gather while a rabbi comes to perform a circumcision.

No hospital. Often not even a doctor or surgeon. Once in a

while, it's a combo rabbi/doctor, but that's a novelty item. This is literally a person who can marry you and is now slicing your son's unit. And what's weird is again—it's happening at a house, an apartment, a local Jewish community center... anywhere OTHER than a medical facility.

So, there you all are, gathering, usually at 8 to 11 a.m. (always morning, it seems), and the mom is usually nowhere to be found. Of course not. Even if she's into it, some rabbi you likely never met is about to do a circumcision on your new pride and joy in front of all your friends and family.

Everyone is gathering, catching up with each other. Lots of mazel tovs and fist bumps going on. And there is little Jacob, wrapped up in some Bris Burrito outfit, ready for some freezing-handed, non-surgeon rabbi to disadvantage his length right out of the gate. He's probably already crying because who wouldn't be? Presuming he knows what's going on.

I can hear Bruce Willis' voice in my head: *Um, so what are all these people doing here, and why is everyone looking at me in this Bris Burrito outfit? I wonder what a bris is. Burritos sound delicious. Why is my grandfather doing shots of Manischewitz this early, and why is my mommy crying and not looking at me?*

Uh oh, they're hoisting me in front of the crowd, showing off my outfit obviously! I'm like Bruce Springsteen with this crowd. They love me. I hope they left some of that bagel and lox for me. Oh, nice, they're laying me down finally. I'm getting exhausted from being shown like a shiny new toy. I'm f-ing cold, dude. Wrap me back up pls! Serves you right. Yup, I'm pissing allll over you cold-hand-dude. Who are you, btw? You don't look like Pappy or Dad or Gramps. What's up with shiny tools that look like we are sitting down to a steak dinner? Are we at Lugers?? Dude... get your f-ing hands off MY peeee...

Olympia Dukakis' voice chiming in...

Umm, yeah, being a boy sucks, dude. How's the Manischewitz, though? I saw Grandpa putting his Manischewitz-soaked pinky in your mouth while that other dude was cutting your manhood.

Seriously though. How is a bris a normal thing?!

I mean, I know it's a cultural thing, but I remember when one of my best friend's wives, who didn't grow up Jewish, was having the bris for her son. She said something to the effect of, "Um Adam, don't you think it's sort of weird that you guys have a non-medical professional perform the circumcision while you all eat bagels and lox?"

I had never heard it put that way. Amazing example of how cultural norms to some are *weird, cult-like shit* to others.

PART SEVEN

THE LIFE PIE

CHAPTER 9

LIVING ON PLANET EARTH

0[56] Mars over Venus any day of the week

Our solar system is made up of a lot of revolving and rotating things. Each planet has a different number of hours in its day. Mars is close to Earth, with approximately 25 hours. But Venus? Each day is 5,832 hours.

We all only get 24 hours a day, 7 days a week, 52 weeks a year. There's no cheat code, albeit AI agents are starting to create those extra hours. You don't get to live on Mars or Venus. So, the real question is always about awareness and intentionality: how you spend your hours, days, weeks, months, and years.

0[57] The Life Pie

Seven years ago, I was talking with a friend who was unusually stressed. He never got rattled. After some digging, I learned he was dealing with major health issues with his wife. Naturally, I assumed that was the root of his stress. But it wasn't. Instead, he talked about all the other things he felt obligated to do: mentoring at work, playing in a men's softball league, chairing a charity event.

The visual of the Life Pie popped into my brain. "Why are you spending time mentoring anyone right now when your wife is having a health crisis?" I asked.

He said things like, "Well, I committed to it," or "This person is counting on me," or "I enjoy giving back."

I looked him straight in the eye and said, "You need to get rid of that piece of your Life Pie. There are only 24 hours in a day. She needs your time. Collapse the mentoring piece. Make it go dormant." I didn't know it then, but that episode was going to shape how I think about Time Wealth and talk about it to others.

0[58] Time wealth

Many of the people I talk with don't fully grasp the finite nature of time until I ask them to draw their Life Pie. Draw a pie to divide up your major activities: work, parenting, fitness, whatever you do during a typical week. Try your best to size the pieces appropriately and label each one. Now, try to add a new pursuit.

Cheryl's 22 Year Old Life Pie

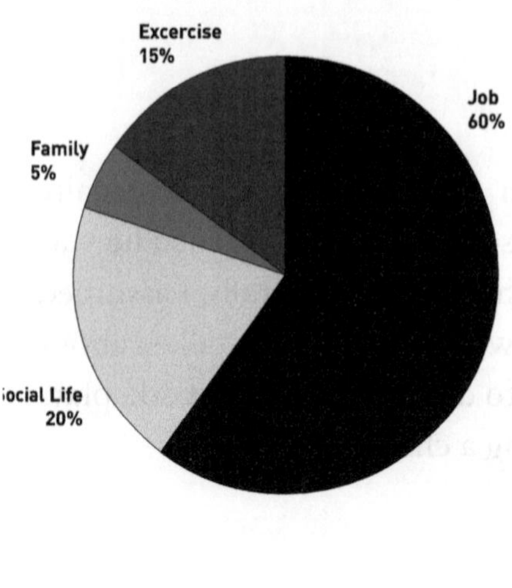

The key insight? Your Life Pie never gets bigger. What does happen is that new entrants appear, and when they do, other pieces, by definition, must shrink.

For Cheryl, 22, just out of college, life's easy. Fun. Uncrowded. Not much competition for her time. She works hard, hits the gym daily, goes out with friends. That's her early-stage Life Pie.

Now fast-forward to Cheryl at 29. She's married to Todd. And she needs to free some time and energy in her life for him. That means other areas must shrink.

- Exercise? Down 5%.
- Social life? Down 10%.
- Work focus? Down 5%.

Cheryl's 29 Year Old Life Pie

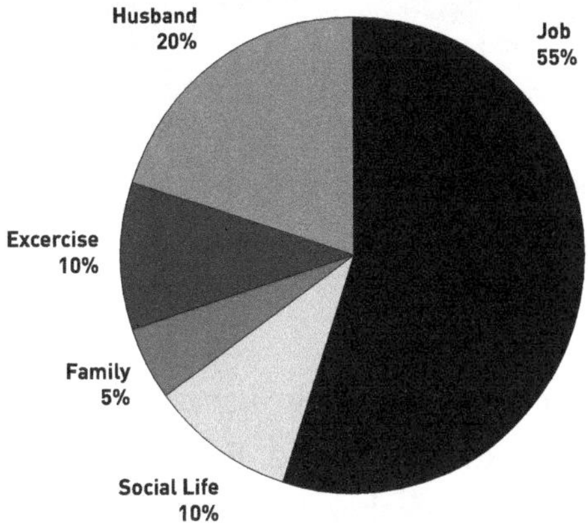

By definition, Todd's existence in Cheryl's life HAD TO come from somewhere. She can't invent time or move to Mars or Venus. Btw, I know men are from Mars and women are from Venus. But now that I've highlighted the 5,832 hours there are in a day on Venus, are you scratching your head, too, about the reason that famous book picked those two planets? Anyway, we also see that her focus on her job went down a bit by 5%. That may or may not be a concern as she looks to rebalance the pie.

0[59] Stuck on Earth

Fast forward a few more years. Cheryl and Todd now have a daughter, Cindy. She's adorable. And she bumped a lot of the other pieces of Cheryl's life almost right out of the pie, rightfully so. Cheryl and Todd now need babysitters and date nights. Life is less spontaneous.

- Exercise? Down to 5%. (From 15% a decade ago!)
- Todd? Steady at 20%.

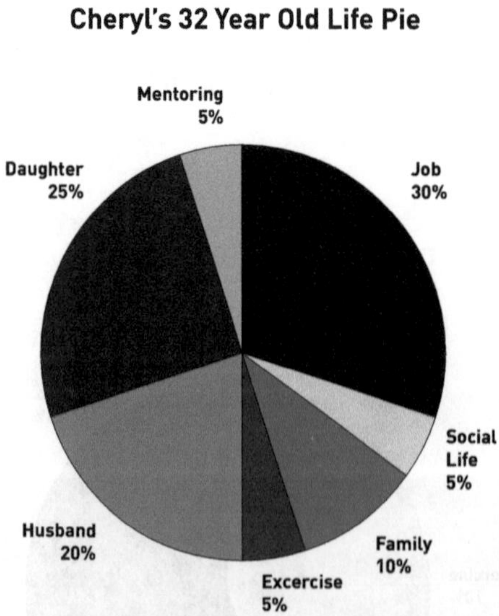

- Family? Up to 10%
- Social life? A consolation prize.

So, let's ask Cheryl: Why are you exercising so little?

How the fuck am I supposed to get to SoulCycle or Barry's Bootcamp, Adam? It's 10–15 minutes each way. The classes are an hour. I used to do both 2x a week. That's 5–6 hours I DEFINITELY don't have anymore!" And the weekend runs? Another hour or so. Unless I move to Venus, those hours are gone.

In Cheryl's mind, Exercise = (2 SoulCycle x 1hr) + (2 Bootcamp x 1hr) + (2 weekend runs x 30min) + (4 round trips x 30min)

That's seven hours a week. But because Cheryl can't find seven hours, she doesn't do this weird thing called exercise very much.

What if instead the equation looked like this?

Exercise =

- Max air squats, 1 min, 4x/day x 7 days
- Push-ups or chair dips, 1 min, 4x/day x 7 days
- Weekend runs, 30 min x 2

In case mental math isn't your thing, that's 116 minutes total. Less than 2 hours.

It's bite-sized, habitual, achievable. And it reinvigorates exercise without consuming more of the Life Pie. You can't add more hours to the day, but there's nothing stopping you from using them more efficiently.

0^{60} Priorities

As life goes on, and your responsibilities mount, it's important to be intentional about the pieces of your Life Pie. Here on Earth, we are constrained by time.

Let's fast forward to Cheryl at 42. She's now also caring for her mom, a big new piece. Too many pieces of Cheryl's life pie are activated. Some need to collapse and lie dormant to make room.

Cheryl now needs to be very intentional about how she is spending her time and effort. She still wants to focus on Todd, her two beautiful kids, her friends, her job and her health. She still needs to do her air squats. Mentoring and PTA are nice-to-haves at this stage, not need-to-haves.

Her updated Life Pie requires:

- Redefining the other side of the equal sign
- Adding new pieces
- Enlarging key areas
- Shrinking old ones
- Letting some go dormant

Cheryl's 42 Year Old Life Pie - Inertial

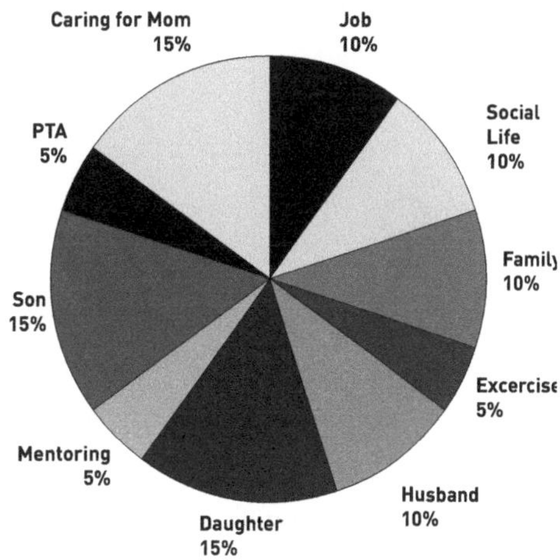

Cheryl's 42 Year Old Life Pie - Intentional

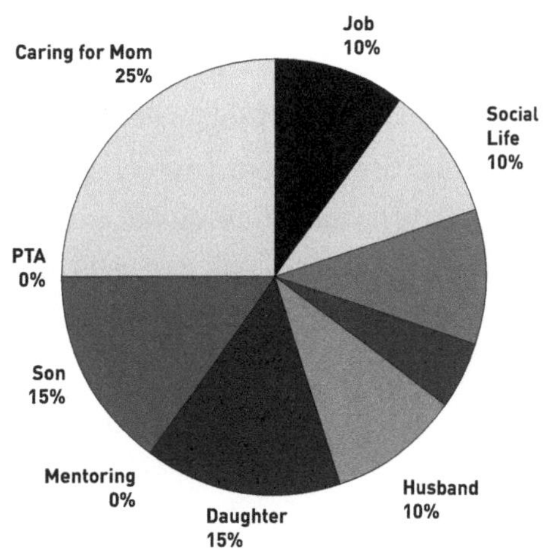

As you think about your own Life Pie, recognize that it will change. New entrants will come. You'll need to redefine priorities. Some slices will need to shrink, while you make room for others.

THE MINDFUL LIFE PIE

No matter how wealthy you are, you can't create more hours in the day. Yes, of course, you can use financial wealth to get back some time, but that's not the point. We all have the same hours in a day and days in a week.

Be mindful of where you are in life and the pieces of your life pie. New ones will emerge and require space. Therefore, other pieces will typically need to shrink. Be mindful of how your life pie is changing throughout different stages of life. Make room for new pieces. Be proactive in discarding some or shrinking them.

Equally important, look for ways to redefine some of them rather than discarding them entirely. Exercise is the easiest example. While you may no longer be able to go on four-hour training runs for a marathon on a Saturday, you can still run. You may not be able to get to the gym five times a week, but you can still do 100,000 push-ups in a year. Stuff like that.

0[61] Back to Merrill

So, let's shift gears into the pre-Gordon Gekko era of business. I started in my training program with Lego-man-like gelled hair in 1998. I still remember faxing things all the time. Man, when that paper clip button suddenly appeared and you could attach documents to an email, it was like the skies opened up and the sun shone on your face.

Now let's go back even a little before this. When no one had cell phones. Forget smartphones, etc. I mean, zero connectivity once you left your "office." Could have been to take a piss. Could have been to grab lunch. Could have been to go to a doctor's appointment. If you weren't at your desk or in your office, either it just rang. And rang. And rang. Until either someone else picked up your phone, OR the other person got tired of waiting for someone to pick up. I suppose "voicemail" came about at some point, but that pretty much would be the same thing as what I'm about to depict.

So, you'd pop out for a lunch meeting when that important call arrived. You'd get back an hour later, and there was a piece of paper, with some likely pre-printed words and corresponding lines telling you about the call you missed, often written in doctor-like cursive letters:

Literally looked like this. Wild. I LOVE the top right "Urgent" box someone could check. There were so many chances for error. Notes might never make it to your desk. They may have fallen off your desk when someone who just delivered the note slammed your door closed behind them, creating a weird wind-like vortex in your office, wafting the paper right off its short-lived home.

And even if you received the note, there was a good chance that names were spelled phonetically, numbers transposed, or even missing. SO many places for error. But let's assume it was all recorded PERFECTLY. Then you needed to call this person back at their office.

And the same thing would happen. "Oh, Mr. Smith is out at an appointment. Can I take a message?" And the work phone tag went on for DAYS. Think about that. What could now be taken care of over email or text in seconds or minutes (and in real time), would span DAYS back then. I'm not sure if that was good or bad, but it's amazing to think about how slow-paced life was in that era.

I have such a vivid memory of when my first boss got his first "crackberry" in 1999. It was the one that looked like a beeper and had only a few lines of text to read.

I thought it was the coolest thing EVER. I couldn't wait to get my own. If I only knew then what we ALL know now. Pre-cell phone life (let alone smartphone) was better in so many ways. We learned to speak to people (especially for those high school dating episodes). We were forced to slow down. Of course, there are many positives from these technologies, but I believe we've lost a bunch, too.

0^{62} The intercom

Okay, so let's go back to the Rite Aids of that era! So, I was there with Dad, coming straight from the doctor's office. Two sections were my favorite back then: The toy aisle and the movie rental area. Yup, a movie rental area. This is obviously WAY before the current form of streaming content or even on demand cable movies. Blockbuster was dominant at this time, but it was WAY more expensive than Rite Aid. I think they let you rent movies for a day for $.89 or something like that. It was definitely under a dollar.

We'll get back to the movie part in a little bit, but I have one specific memory of a toy I got at that Rite Aid when I was sick. It was a set of two plastic "cups" connected by a 20-foot string. It said on the packaging something about communicating with your friends in another room in secret. I'm guessing a lot of you remember what I'm talking about.

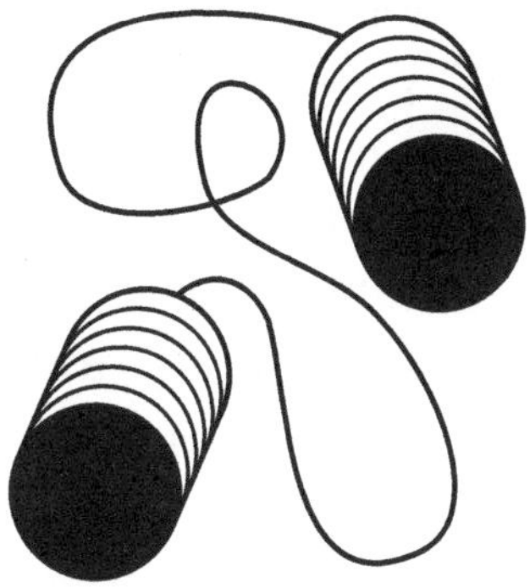

That gave me a seemingly brilliant idea. I was going to create an intercom system for my house with this concept!! So, I got home and literally created an entire setup for my upstairs.

To be clear, this was a very, very modest split-level home. There were four "bedrooms" (mine was 10'x10' for a visual, with brown jungle wallpaper), but I set up a spaghetti string "system" across the entire upstairs. Everyone's room had a cup sitting on the floor in the doorway, and the strings were strewn across the brown plush carpet in the hallways. Mind you, my brother's room was LITERALLY next to mine. Like, his doorway was adjacent and perpendicular to mine (think of two sides of a square). I could literally have one foot in my doorway while having one foot in his, even when I was probably 4'6." I could probably jump to my sister's doorway with a decent running start not available to me in my 10'x10' room with a twin bed. And my parents' doorway was probably 15' away. It was a great time for imagination back then. Forget real intercoms. Nowadays, I FaceTime my kids in my own house. Speaks less to size and more to the way life is today. Anyone see Wall-E?

Two people sitting right next to each other, talking to each other, but through a smart device. Not actually talking to each other. Definitely an extreme example but can't help but mention we are heading this way faster than I could have imagined when I saw *Wall-E* for the first time.

0[63] The sore throat

So, the morning I went to the Rite Aid, I had woken up with a revelation: "I can't believe I have a fucking sore throat. I feel awful. Why me!" Now, here's the interesting perspective I want to share. How many mornings a YEAR do you think you wake up with a sore throat? Five? Seven? Ten?

When I asked myself this question many years ago, it occurred to me that I never woke up the other 355 to 360 days a year and said, "Morning world, I feel amazing this morning. My throat doesn't ache at all."

It made me realize that we naturally have this wildly emotional imbalance in the things we notice and the things we do not. Rationally, we should observe all the perceived positive things, but instead, our brains are wired the opposite way. How often do you get to your destination on a road trip and say, "Man, super psyched I didn't get a flat tire or get into an accident!" Never is my guess.

This type of daily stuff, around getting a sore throat, getting a flat tire, stubbing my toe while walking around my bedroom and similar, got me thinking: Why aren't we wired to notice all the times the "bad stuff" DOESN'T happen…and have mini celebrations about how "well" daily life goes.

Now this is the completely privileged, developed, first-world version, but for simplicity, let's just keep it in that zone. So, I started observing life at a young age through a very different lens, recognizing a lot of the daily parts of life that go just as planned. No bumps in the proverbial road. No sore throats. Just life without speedbumps.

SORE THROAT PARADOX

How many days do you wake up with a sore throat a year? Exactly. Not many. Spend time every day embracing all the good that is happening: Waking up feeling amazingly healthy. Your body working well. Relationships humming. This is a spin on "don't take things for granted," but I think the "sore throat" concept really exemplifies the concept even better. I often say that we all win good and bad lotteries. But we tend to focus a disproportionate amount of time on counting the bad ones we win, not the good ones. Be mindful of this, and your days will become infinitely more enjoyable. When someone asks you, "How are you doing?" your answer should never be "fine." It should be "fucking awesome." Because, thru this lens, I'm sure it is.

PART EIGHT

MANAGERS, LEADERS AND MENTORS, OH MY!

CHAPTER 10

MANAGEMENT POTENTIAL

0[64] Who's in charge?

The months between my junior and senior years in college were eventful and formative. I stayed in Boston that summer, probably the first one I hadn't been at my sleepaway summer camp in a good decade, as either a camper or a counselor. I was the worst counselor. In many ways, a counselor SHOULD act more like a manager, but I tended to trend more like a mentor. Definitely not a leader. Those are the three roles that I talk about a lot when explaining the journey in a career.

If you think about it, these three are VERY different, but often get fully jumbled up in the blender and spit out as sort of the same goop with indiscernible qualities. A manager does what that sounds like: Manages people. Instructs. Holds people accountable. Sets your schedule and priorities. Tells you if you're great (or suck). "Manager" has a negative connotation, not quite in the same category as the in-laws. If you are lucky, you think the manager you have is "good."

It is interesting how the "in-laws" negative connotation tends to hold true a lot. Movies about this shit are funny for a reason: they're pretty relatable, albeit hyperbolized. I mean, none of us is really playing pool volleyball in a borrowed Speedo, but Meet the

Parents did a great job of showing an exaggerated version of the first meeting with future in-laws.

"If Florence Nightingale would play a little defense!" "JC was a carpenter, too!" "How's your portfolio, Greg?" "Strong to quite strong." Okay, moving on, but holy shit, those are some of the best movie lines ever.

The point is, saying "The in-laws are in town this weekend" tends to be met by a sigh. And like in-laws, you can't pick and choose managers. You may suddenly get the knock on your sea-of-office-cubicle door frames and learn that you have a new manager (if you didn't get the 411 in an e-mail blast). But looking at this from a different lens, managers tend to inherit a team they didn't pick, so they're probably just as surprised to be working with you. Regardless, it's wise to keep in mind that these relationships are not long term. Your "manager" is rarely a person you'll think about and talk about in 5, 10 or 20 years in the future.

A leader. Now, this is a little to a lot different from a manager (who could be the same person, but often is not). This is someone you want to go into battle with…or more specifically, FOR. Leaders inspire you. You listen to their every word. You watch their every action. You fantasize about being them. You may or may not work for them or with them. In fact, they may not even know your name. But you know theirs. Everyone does. Gladiator's Maximus (a very in-shape Russell Crowe) didn't know every man in his army, but every man in his army knew him. THAT is a leader.

Now, let's get to a mentor. Mentors can be your boss but they often are not. Mentors are advisors you look up to. Perhaps you love their presentation style. Maybe you love their shoes.

Anyway, you admire their smarts. You watch their political moves. They inspire you. You want to be them in some way. They're different from leaders because there is an actual relationship. They know you;

you know them. You spend time together. But, unlike your manager, they almost ALWAYS pick you. Forget dumb formal "mentor" programs. I'm talking about the organic shit. The mentors who find you in a crowd, at cocktail hour, in a gym class, in a cafeteria, or in a boardroom meeting. They're just folks you meet, or who meet you, and begin spending time in a friendship of sorts; what's different is there is a teacher/pupil dynamic, a clear hierarchy of who's mostly doing the talking and who's mostly listening. We tend to have fond memories of our mentors over a lifetime. But again, the most crucial part of all this is that mentors PICK their mentees.

MANAGERS, LEADERS, MENTORS

Usually, we find ourselves in roles that someone else has given to us, rather than simply finding our way into them organically. Be mindful of the different roles you'll see in most organizations and how they play out: Managers often inherit folks they didn't want. Leaders tend to emerge; they aren't appointed. We typically only mentor people we really like.

In the office, focus on what you like and are best at. Don't conflate these things. I'd imagine most people reading this will gravitate to mentorship, then leadership and then management. In your personal life, remember that family and friends likely don't want to be managed. Or perhaps even led. Maybe they want to be mentored, at best.

0[65] Leadership lessons from camp

A camp counselor's first and primary job is to be a manager and THEN to potentially inspire and lead the campers. And perhaps the manager builds some strong relationships with some of the campers and serves as a mentor, especially as they get older.

I learned early in life, as a camp counselor, that I was way more interested in being a mentor than a manager. And as such, I sorta skipped over the most basic job requirement and simply picked favorites. Simple as that. As a manager of the bunk, I inherited a bunch of kids to manage for the summer. I didn't like a lot of them, so I simply skipped over most and went right to my favorites and just mentored a few.

One ridiculous thing I remember doing was bringing back a bacon cheeseburger for my favorite camper one night. Now, on the surface, I'm guessing this doesn't seem THAT weird. But let's dig in a bit here. Our camp was a Jewish camp. Depending on where you live, you may be like, "Aren't all camps Jewish?" at this point. As we discussed, it is a weird cultural norm for Jews to send their kids away all summer.

Anyway, so this was a RELIGIOUS Jewish camp. I'm talking, praying every morning, where boys 13 and over, who have had their Bar Mitzvah, are supposed to wrap tefillin. (TUH-FILL-IN is how you pronounce that. What are TUH-FILL-IN you might ask–even many of you Berg's and Stein's reading this) … it's these:

So, back to the bacon cheeseburger. The camp was clearly kosher. I mean, we made ourselves look like we were in a cult every morning. Of course, the camp was kosher. In the hierarchy of Jewish customs and traditions, being kosher was nothing compared to the Jews wrapping TUH-FILL-IN.

So, there I was, out at night with my fellow counselor friends. To be clear, when I went back to be a counselor, I clearly didn't go back to be the "manager" type of counselor. I was definitely not the "leader" type, trying to inspire other counselors on how to do the "job" or campers to want to be counselor one day. At BEST, I went in with this whole mentor mindset. Again, that's just a fancy way of saying I talked to the kids I liked. My favorites. In this case, singular, favorite. I don't even know if he had any friends in the bunk because he was much cooler than the rest.

But there I was, with my own buddies, probably at the Ground Round. Does that even exist anymore? I gotta tell the steak story at the Ground Round. I heard them order a steak in this weird preparation called "medium rare." Didn't really pay attention, but I do remember the words being uttered. I was probably paying attention more than an 18- or 19-year-old kid would today, because we had no phones.

So, our meals came. I don't recall what I ordered, but I looked at my friend's hunk of meat and was confused. What is this medium-rare-steak-thing you ordered? I asked myself, and then was like, "Hey, can I get a bite?"

It was as if the heavens had opened up. As we have covered, my family was kosher. I had only eaten kosher meat my whole life. This was NOT kosher meat. In fact, it was a cut that's rarely possible to get in a kosher version, filet mignon! (I know, it was unlikely the Ground Round had the real deal, but just go with it for the story's sake.)

There I was, in the Ground Round, and my life's never been the same. It was juicy. It was salty and flavorful. It WASN'T medium well plus, as I'm guessing my dad would have ordered if we were ever at a steakhouse, based on how he prepared any steak we had at our house, which was a very occasional thing. I'm not even sure I'd ever seen any moisture or leakage on the plate below what my dad called a steak. It was this very oddly colored, leathery hunk that I needed to muscle chew my way through. It always got stuck in my teeth. I mean, like EVERY. SINGLE. TOOTH.

I definitely didn't use dental floss as a kid, so I probably just dealt with it. Although perhaps I used the *TV Guide* like my Nana. No joke, after a Friday night dinner at my house when Nana came over, we'd inevitably all make our way down to the temple in my house (i.e., the family room) to watch some Friday night programming. Nana would always sit behind us in the corner nook with a table, a dangling lamp and a couple of chairs. She'd be there with the *TV Guide*, and I'd eventually hear the ripping of the pages (not sure what section she favored).

And then, if I wanted, I could turn around and take a break from Friday night programming and see her flossing with the freshly torn *TV Guide* section. Yes, she would literally slide the somewhat glossed paper page in between her not-so-pristine-to-start-with teeth, to dislodge something my mom or dad had cooked to death that evening for dinner. Could have actually been this leather steak I speak of. Could have been the crumbliest, flakiest corned beef you've ever seen (I know, you'd think with my last name, my dad would know how to steam some corned beef…it's like he picked the "dehydrate" setting on some cooking apparatus). Flossing with the *TV Guide*. Love you, Nana!

Oh, and the mustard. My dad would spread yellow mustard on top of a steak as a finishing touch. Dry, brown, dehydrated, mustard-finished steak. It wasn't this Ground Round masterpiece that I devoured once I got a taste of my buddy's that night!

Anyway, so flashing back to the bacon cheeseburger night. We get back to camp. Now, realize that the way it worked is that once your campers went to bed (or at least you told them to), you got to "check out" for the night with the "security" team for the evening. This was essentially two counselors a night who had to sort of walk around the side of the camp to make sure the campers were fine. That's a stretch at best, meaning you pretty much walked around the side of the camp a couple of times in a few hours, and unless anyone was screaming or crying, you quickly made your way back to the office of sorts that served as the headquarters. So, you'd "check out" with them and then "check in" by like 1 a.m. It was crazy. Never would happen this way anymore.

Besides being the worst counselor that summer, there was one night when I was "checking out" that I was told I couldn't leave quite yet. My bunk was still making noise, all the way across the field where the headquarters were. I looked at the boss who told me I couldn't leave yet and probably wanted to smash them (I mean, I was there to hang with my friends every night, not be an actual counselor), and said, "Okay, I'll be right back." So, I started making my way over the bunk.

Now, for a visual, I was a pretty muscular guy at this point (especially when you throw that muscularity on a curve for a religious Jewish summer camp...I mean, the muscularity in our DNA seems to mostly have been omitted from the genetic code). Anyway, I was fired up. My friends were waiting for me to go to the Ground Round or something similar probably, and I'd been delayed.

So, I walked into my bunk (probably slammed the door open loudly and angrily) and started yelling at them. I don't know what I said. Who remembers? I just know it had a lot of "fucks" and was loud. The general theme was "Shut the fuck up long enough for me to get cleared by security so I can go out with my friends and then do whatever the fuck you want after." General theme. Loud.

Done with my tirade, I busted out that same door, backed down the creaking wooden stairs, onto the root-laden dirt path that went around the perimeter of that field I'd just crossed, and there stood my bosses. The people who ran my division. Their mouths were open. No words came out. They just stared at me. I don't remember much after that evening (I didn't black out or anything. I literally just have zero clue what happened). I "think" I still actually went to the Ground Round, but recounting that story, I'd imagine they probably had a talk with me and didn't let me go out that night.

Which brings us back to the Bacon Cheeseburger Episode. We got back from the Ground Round one night, and I had a bacon cheeseburger. I'd imagine I didn't try to hide it, because where would a person hide one? It was a hot-as-balls-summer-camp-with-no-AC situation…so I'm guessing I had a T-shirt and shorts on.

Hopefully, I wasn't wearing Tevas or Birks and exposing my man toes. Literally one of the worst things we humans must look at is men's toes. Anyway, so I made my way to the bunk and woke my favorite camper in the middle of the night and asked him to come to the bathroom with me. He was clearly confused, and, in retrospect, G-d knows what he thought I wanted. Ummmmm. Anyway, he made his way to the bathroom, still sorta sleeping, and I'm like, "Voila, here's a lukewarm, soggy bacon cheeseburger I got for you, my favorite camper. Zero clue if you're kosher or even like this thing, but I somehow thought this was a good idea and now I'm going to awkwardly make this a bonding experience." Wow.

Again, in my mind, I was a mentor. He wasn't looking for one or asking for one, but he was my favorite. I didn't want to manage the bunk. I wanted to find a mentee! Needless to say, I was NOT asked back as a counselor for the following summer.

0^{66} Post-summer-camp counselor

Getting back to the summer between my junior and senior year in college, my girlfriend was back home in South Africa, BUT she left me her car. Understand, I love cars. But back then, I didn't have one. In fact, I didn't get my own until I was 24. Lexus IS 300 back in 2000. It was a hot car, albeit my now-wife Dana mocked me when she met me, thinking I had some old man's car. Story for another time.

So, it was the summer of '97, and I had my girlfriend's white two-door Chevy Cavalier. I think, based on my own experience with cars in my family (Chevy Eurosport, Caprice Classics and Taurus), this thing looked and felt pretty sporty! I didn't feel cool driving this thing around, but it was wheels. It was freedom. It sorta felt like mine.

And it gave me the mobility to have a couple of jobs and internships that summer. This was the semester after I had my Merrill Lynch internship in downtown Boston. So, I had again made my way to the White Pages under Financial Services and found a smaller firm. They needed an intern, and they were going to PAY me. Remember, I was coming off the now-would-not-fly internship where I got paid nothing. Literally nothing. No money. No credits. He did pay for my train pass, but that was it.

But here I was, a few months later, it was summer, and I had wheels. So, I got the gig through some phone interviews, and I was on my way to the suburban office. Think it was like 30 minutes north of Waltham, where I lived at that time. I made my way there for my first day, probably wearing a Sy Syms suit and the whole ensemble. I think my official title was "marketing coordinator." I had a whole plan and narrative already. "Well, once I had the big firm experience at Merrill Lynch during my junior year, the following summer I thought it would be smart to contrast that with a boutique firm where I could have an even greater impact." Yes, I was always using my time machine in my head.

So, I got there the first day, looking for my new business cards with "marketing coordinator" and my actual name (contrasted with the Kurt…just Kurt, with no last name, like Cher, business cards in my pocket for my club promoting job) and an office, of course! Alas, no business cards, no office and definitely no "marketing coordinating."

Remember that phone book I used to find my "financial services" jobs? They pretty much gave me the same one and said, "Start with the As. For any meeting you get me, I'll give you $50. If they become a client, I'll give you $250." Not sure if those were the exact numbers, but you get the gist.

I was meant to be a cold caller. I was told to start calling at 6 p.m. because that's when most people are eating dinner. Soooo… I was 20 years old, knew nothing about anything, and I was supposed to interrupt people's dinners and get them to talk to me about what exactly? Yeah, that lasted about a day. I quit quickly.

Back to the phone book. I did end up getting an internship at a local Smith Barney office, but that was mostly about doing weird things for the woman I was interning for. She was a financial advisor. Ex-teacher nice.

Once she asked me and another intern to go to her car and bring a fancy Vornado fan into her office. She was always very hot. In hindsight, probably going through menopause. In any case, something happened that summer where she barely came in. Which essentially meant that I didn't have to come in. But I got paid. I was like. "This is amazing!!" Interestingly, the other intern still came in. To this day, we remain friendly and are actually sorta in the same industry. He'll still mention, as a frame of reference, that he still came in and worked every day, and I didn't, but we both got paid the same amount. Formative shit!

PART NINE

CHEESECAKE

CHAPTER 11

CREATURES OF THE NIGHT

0^{67} All black

Okay, I was getting paid for doing nothing, and I needed to occupy my time. So, I went to the local mall in my white Chevy Cavalier and started walking around to see if any of the stores were hiring. I eventually made my way into the Cheesecake Factory. I had never worked at a restaurant before. They had an opening as a "host." I could do that. They agreed.

I started the next day. I think I had to wear all black, so my wardrobe was perfect, plus suitable for my night job, too. I worked at a nightclub in downtown Boston as a quasi-bouncer. I say quasi because I didn't do a lot of bouncing. In fact, if a fight broke out, I'd go to the bathroom and pretend I was having diarrhea. Every time. I guess there weren't enough fights to make this look like a pattern, but yes, I would quite literally pretend to shit myself if a fight broke out.

I also used to love going to this club to dance. I was in a major "eurotrash" phase. I literally walked around with platform shoes, a silver jacket and matching sunglasses. Very gelled hair. By the way, I would wear that type of outfit everywhere. When my brother and sister visited me in college, we'd go to downtown Boston and specifically walk on Newbury Street. Everyone would look at me. I thought back then that they envied my cool look!

0[68] Do I look like a valet?

So, it was one of my first Sundays at the Cheesecake Factory during the brunch rush. Some dude walked right up to the host stand where my fellow hosts and I were the keepers of the list ("Oh, that will be a two-hour wait. Would you like a beeper, and you can go shopping while you wait?") to get a table.

The guy looked at me: "Hey, can you do me a favor? That's my car outside. If it starts raining, please come and get me."

I walked outside. Parked front and center with the valet team was a Bentley convertible. I don't think I'd ever seen one before. As a kid, I still thought a doctor or lawyer was rich. A Mercedes was the top of the heap in my town. But holy shit, a fucking Bentley convertible! I was in awe.

So, lo and behold, a little later, it started raining. I quickly found this guy and proudly tapped him on the shoulder. "Sir, it's started to rain, so I wanted to let you know right away so that your interior wouldn't get wet." I don't recall exactly what happened next, but I remember the handshake. He came and found me, looked me in the eye and said, "Thanks, I really appreciate that you came to get me," as he simultaneously shook my hand.

And then I felt it. Not a tickly, weird finger or anything like that. Although that was oddly part of my secret fraternity handshake, and probably most people's. I remember when that same friend, with the wad of $100 bills, gave me the secret handshake with the tickly finger insert, and I looked at him with disbelief. He was in ZBT; I was in AEPi. How did he know MY fraternity's secret handshake?

"Adam, did you really think the handshakes were any different?" he asked. "Only so many things you can do with five fingers."

Okay, so back to THIS handshake. There was something in his hand. I had never gotten THIS type of handshake but, of course, I had seen it in movies and stuff. Remember, my family didn't really have money, so I NEVER saw Dad do a handshake like this with anyone.

I calmly and seemingly coolly said, "Thank you, no problem," and didn't look, but slipped whatever was just placed in my hand into my pocket. I quickly told my fellow black-clad-host-mafia that I needed to run to the bathroom. Not with the diarrhea excuse I relied on when a fight broke out, but a run-of-the-mill-I-gotta-pee vibe.

I made it to the bathroom and into the stall. I'm a stall guy anyway, but I wanted some privacy for the unveiling. I reached into my pocket, removed this square-folded greenback and looked at the top left corner. Guesses?

$1. Yes, I didn't forget to add some zeros. This motherfucker gave me $1. I had hoped for a twenty, fantasized about a hundred. It confused, angered and surprised me. And unknowingly, it helped shape one of my formative concepts that lay dormant for almost 30 years. I affectionately refer to it as Random Acts of Daily Financial Kindness.

0[69] 20%?

So, one of the ways I used to teach my kids math was during our Saturday and Sunday morning breakfasts. Once my oldest (now 20) was four or five, I started taking him to breakfast most Saturday and Sunday mornings. Eventually, when his sis was the same age (they're about four years apart), I'd take her, too. I loved the idea of it, but the execution typically led to them battling in some way. Dana always asked why I did it. Answer is obvious regarding memory making, etc. We did this til my son was prob 14/15, and then it sorta died out. We still go a bunch, but with less regularity and often one-on-one, rarely the three of us. Miss those days.

So, as they grew old enough to do some basic math, I taught them how to calculate a tip. It's always weird to me how people can't do mental math. This isn't me being a dick or arrogant, it's just hard when your brain works a certain way to fathom how others don't. Again, this isn't an elitist-I'm-Mr.-Mensa type of comment. Mental math is just something I get that many others don't. Especially around tipping at a restaurant, especially before they brought around the machines with the tip percentage and tip amount, and you just needed to press a button. Cheating!!!

Okay, back to the diner breakfasts. So, a bill would come, and it would be $30, and I'd say, "What do you think the tip is?" In the beginning, I'd need to remind them that it's customary to tip 20% for good service. So, they'd grab a crayon from the diner's crayon cup (iPads weren't a thing yet, or at least we hadn't bought one).

They'd do some scribbling and I'd inevitably, because I can't unsee what I see in my brain, blurt the words "Just THINK about it." I'd push them and say, "Well, what's 10%?"

Eventually, I'd get the "30 cents?" I'd add some gibberish about "Move the decimal," etc. (I'd be an awful math teacher.) Then they'd get to $3.

"Okay, great. Sooooooo...what is 20% then?"

It would always take a little longer than I expected to get to the seemingly impossibly easy math concept of "If $3 is 10%, and 20% is double 10%, then obviously the 20% tip is double the $3, so it's $3x2=$6." My brain could (and candidly still) can't get how this isn't instinctive to people. Bill is $125? 20% Tip is $25. Bill is $350. 20% tip is $70. Don't get how this doesn't jump out at people. And THAT is, of course, why I could never TEACH math, even though I GET it and love it.

But I'm back in the Cheesecake Factory. And I recall the $1 bill. That was clearly the wrong number. Not sure what the right one is/was. I'm good at the mental math on 20%. My kids are good at the mental math of 20%. Mental tip math, like memorizing phone numbers, has essentially gone away with technology. Screens on those mobile payment devices look like this:

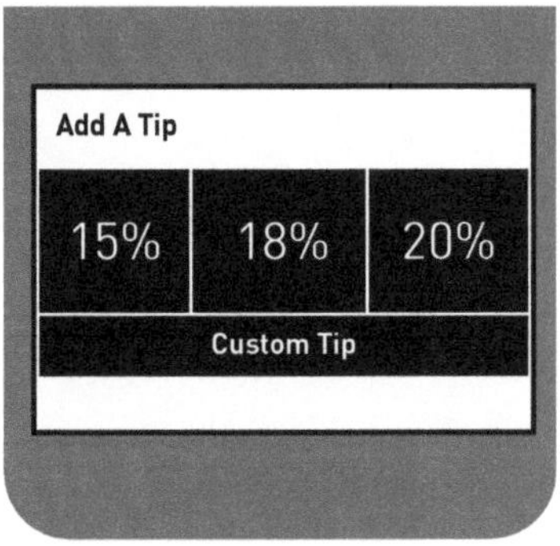

Okay, yes, my mental math for a 20% tip would be rounding to $19, and not $19.14, but mental math is a lost art. But, more importantly, WHY 20%?

CHAPTER 12

TIPPING WITH THE ZEROS IN MIND

0^{70} Table real estate

I was sitting with my daughter at a nice, trendy restaurant a few years ago, which was a carrot for her if she got straight As. I had brought her brother to this restaurant a couple of years earlier, and she'd been begging to go. She'd gotten all fancy. She was probably 12, and TikTok had influenced her outfit, makeup, and where to take insta pics IN the restaurant she'd never been to. Amazing.

Setting the stage, she and I were sitting at our table. We ordered and had a great meal, and then the check came. I'm not sure exactly what happened, but I had an epiphany: Here we were. At a great trendy restaurant. Prime time. Prime seat. And when I went to grab the leather booklet that housed the check for this meal, I was looking at the two empty seats across from me.

No, this isn't some sad tangent about her dead grandparents who could have been with us to celebrate (wow, interesting that I went there as an example, as I suppose in some ways, I wish they were sitting there, but that isn't the point at all). I am simply saying we weren't seated at a table for two. We were seated at a table for four. It's a nice restaurant, so figure the bill was something like this:

Pellegrino - $12
Sprite - $8
Don Julio 1942 (2) - $110
Tuna tartare - $32
Caesar salad - $22
Petit filet - $45
Cowboy - $65
Crème brûlée - $14
Subtotal - $308
Tax - $12
Total - $320

Mental math can't help but unsee the number $64. Adam, just write that number on the tip line, total it to $384, sign some deteriorated version of your name, which looks like a hieroglyphic, and stand up and leave.

But it didn't sit right with me. Something was all wrong. Why was I tipping 20% on the bill? I couldn't unsee the $1 bill in the Cheesecake Factory bathroom, nor could I unsee those two empty seats in our four top.

So, I got to thinking: Why was my waiter getting penalized for the fact that the host (prob much cooler, and better-looking, and better-dressed than I was at the Cheesecake Factory) sat a dad and his 12-year-old daughter out on a straight-A celebratory dinner at her four-top real estate? I thought to myself, what if instead of the two of us, it was my wife and I and our best couple friends celebrating someone's promotion, a milestone birthday, or really anything a suburban crew would use as an excuse to celebrate (talk about eventisizing!).

So, I used my calculator brain and played a quick game. First, I thought to myself, well, here I am with my 12-year-old daughter so two things are happening: 1. She wasn't drinking any alcohol as that would be weird and not legal. 2. I was inclined to drink way less with her because drinking more would just be strange, and I also drove into the city from the NJ burbs, so I needed to stay very sober and safe. Also, she was 12. She didn't eat that much. We weren't sharing lots of appetizers and desserts.

So, let's see...what do I think the bill would have looked like in that alternate universe where we came into the city with our besties and took an Uber, of course? How about this:

Pellegrino (3) - $36
Rosé (bottle) - $125
Don Julio 1942 (6) - $330
Seafood tower - $200
Tuna tartare - $32
Tomahawk - $250
Petit filet (2) - $90
Broccoli - $16
Truffle fries - $16
Brussels sprouts - $16
Crème brûlée - $14
Molten chocolate cake - $14
Cappuccino (2) - $16
Subtotal - $1,100 (okay, I know it's not actually eleven hundered even, but I said I was doing mental math to make the point) – it's exactly $1,155 – fuck, my mental math rounding is getting rusty, but close enough.

Fuck the tax, irrelevant for my point and epiphany.

In that scenario, we would have left a $220 tip. Right, 20% on $1,100? Easy. Scribbled our numbers and names and got on our way.

This confused me.

It was the same table. The same real estate. Why was my waitress making $64 instead of $220? Ohhhhhh, because of the bill?

This didn't sit right with me. Forget the percentage difference, obviously, like 400% or 4x. It's literally a $160 difference (invoke the 3-Digit Rule and Unitization of Money Carries!). Because I came with my daughter instead of my wife and friends? So, I went "custom," and I wrote $200 on the tip line, added it to the $320 total, and the $520 sat on the last line. I told my daughter it was time to head home, and off we went.

I didn't stay to see any reaction. In fact, I tried to leave the restaurant as quickly as possible. I know, most people are trying to do their own mental math, and yes, that's like a 60% tip on $320. But I didn't and DON'T think of it that way. I simply thought about tipping through a new construct that helped shape a much more defined one that I use to this day.

This is one of the most pivotal and foundational moments I had for my idea on Random Acts of Daily Financial Kindness.

RANDOM ACTS OF DAILY FINANCIAL KINDNESS

Every day is an opportunity to use your financial wealth in a way that will impact someone else in a meaningful way. Have a plan here. Think about the different people you run into each day. A valet. Someone who is checking your coat. A bellhop. The team at the car wash. A friend running a marathon. Someone delivering a new fridge to your house. Be prepared. Have a philosophy. Take action. The joy you'll get out of surprising people daily will provide a dopamine hit unlike almost anything else. And holy shit, it will provide real perspective. And if you have kids, tell them about it and why you are doing it.

0[71] The cookie jar

My tipping construct starts like this. No matter what the bill is, my *minimum* tips are organized around parts of the day:

- Coffee (think Dunkin', Starbucks, local spot) - $10 (yes, $10 on your $3 coffee or $7 latte)
- Breakfast: $25 (think diner, local breakfast spot, IHOP, Waffle House)
- Lunch: $50 (think sit down, could be a diner or someplace similar, but not a fast casual place)
- Dinner: $100 (any sit-down place, except somewhere like Chipotle)
- Drink at a Bar: $25 (even if I'm by myself and the drink is $20)

To play this out, let's say I'm with the kids at that same diner, and the check is $30. I don't do the mental math and leave the $6. I leave $25. Yup, almost a 100% tip!

That's not how I think about it. I simply believe that it's an act of kindness that this server does not expect. What's interesting is that it's not $25 more. It's $19 more. Remember, you were going to give $6 anyway, not $0.

So, let's have some fun. How many times do you go to a sit-down breakfast a year? I was obviously doing it a ton when the kids were young, but I'd imagine most people reading this don't even do it once a week. But let's get extreme. I'll give you twice a week. Let's estimate 100x per year. Nineteen extra dollars times 100 breakfasts = $1,900/year of "extra tips."

Now, let's imagine I put it differently on January 1, and said, "Hey Jen, would you brighten up the day (or week) of 100 people for nineteen hundred bucks?" I "get" the financial privilege baked into this example, although this book is geared to help tens to hundreds of thousands of people I'll never meet...and transcends some wealth levels, but not all.

But I'd imagine most people reading this can't tell me down to $1,900 what they have in their proverbial bank account. In fact, I'd imagine most can't tell me down to $190,000 what they have in their proverbial bank account. That's the 3-digit rule in effect!

Remember the Unitization of Money concept? It's super related to the Random Acts of Daily Financial Kindness, but let's stay on this for a moment. For most of you, the $1,900 unit has zero utility. In fact, you can't even see it in your bank account. But think about the massive utility it has to these 100 people every year.

Let's jump to dinner. So, I'm sure you're saying, "Well, Adam, you say $100 minimum for dinner, but then in your example with your daughter on the $320 bill, you left $200 when $100 still would have been really nice and unexpected and more than the $64 tip?" Yeah, the short of it is it's as fun as hell to ramp this shit up. So, let's get into it.

Let's assume a lot of folks reading this think their average dinner check with their spouse or buddy is $250. I'm sure for some that seems super low, for some super high, but it's helpful for my example, so we're gonna use it.

So, using the conventional math my five-year-old kids could apply, 20% of $250 is $50 tip. Scribble, scribble the hieroglyphics and we're on our way. But DOUBLE that EVERY time, Adam, up to $100? An extra $50! A 40% tip? I'm in the "custom" zone every time now on those new credit card machines!

Let's do the math again. How many times do you go out to dinner a year? I'll give you three times a week this time. Always rounding for 50 weeks, that's 150 times a year. 150 times the extra 50 bucks each time, and it's $7,500/year. I know, that's a lot more than the $1,900 you've already spent tipping your waiter all year long at Waffle House.

But same thing. Can you tell me down to $7,500 how much is sitting in your proverbial bank account right now? ZERO. FUCKING. CHANCE. It has no utility to you sitting in your account, but you can make the day/week of 150 servers that year by porting some of your numerator onto all their individual denominators each evening. It's powerful. It's fun. It should be the way we think. At least directionally.

I estimate I spend an extra $30,000-$40,000 per year to surprise and delight hundreds of people. I fortunately am in a position where I don't know down to a $40,000 unit what is in my proverbial bank account. It has no utility to my family. But I know that by using it every day in a different manner, it can make the days/weeks/months of many people better.

While I explained that my goal is to leave the restaurant as soon as possible after the scribble is done, once in a while, I get caught when I'm elbow deep in the cookie jar. Now, this is the good kind of getting caught in the scheme of things, but it usually happens when someone in your party forgets something, needs to pee last minute, the check comes a bit early, or they take the check before you get up, etc.

0[72] Cinco de Mayo

So, here I was at a local Mexican restaurant on Cinco de Mayo a few years ago. They had an adjacent tent set up to handle the big crowd for the day. My buddies, Mike and Chris, and I got there around 9:30 p.m. We found a spot outside under the tent. I looked around before they arrived and saw tables that looked like an encampment. They clearly had been there for hours. I don't think there was some Buffalo Wild Wings all-you-can-eat situation going on, but people definitely had been in for the long haul.

The waitress came over once my buddies arrived and asked what we wanted to drink. This was a local spot in suburban NJ, but they had a super high-end tequila selection. So, I ordered my favorite, the Don Julio 1942. She looked at me like I was an asshole, and in a frazzled tone said, "Uh…, I don't think we have that, it's really busy today, uhhh…." I jumped in and said, "No worries, just let me know what you guys have." She came back and, in a way less frazzled tone, with a hint of apology sprinkled in, and updated me. "Hi, so I checked, and we have that tequila. But it's $32."

Now, I knew from the way she said it, she (a) thought that was ridiculous, (b) had never served it and (c) assumed I'd say "No, thanks." But this is my book, and I simply said, "Thanks so much for checking and for letting me know the price. And I'd still love to get that one. Thanks!"

Fast forward to the end of the night, and the total bill was around \$150. Lots of nachos, some wings, drinks, etc. Standard fare. So, mental math for the 20% club leads to a \$30 tip, scribble, scribble and off we go.

But I knew she had a long day. I also knew the encampment crowd was likely stiffing her, even though they essentially became an unwanted tenant for the day in some of her real estate. So, I left a \$150 tip. Scribble, scribble and Jesus, Chris needs to pee. His parents also ordered him a mini bladder on the genetic scantron, so this happened a lot to us. AND she took the leather folder with \$150 scribbled onto the tip line, unbeknownst to me, while Chris said he'd be right back.

So, I was chatting with Mike, assuming that the check with the \$150 tip was sitting next to me undiscovered, when I suddenly felt someone come up behind me and grab my shoulders. I thought it was Chris coming back from the bathroom, but it was our waitress. I looked over my shoulder, and before I could do or say anything, she looked at me and said a couple of sentences that are etched in my brain. It was simple and powerful. "I don't know how to thank you…my KIDS don't know how to thank you." For \$120 extra, I impacted this woman and her family's life.

I have several other versions of this type of story, where I got my hand caught in the cookie jar, but, hopefully, this will start to shape your own different tipping construct for service workers. And think broadly. A valet at a restaurant. A valet at a hotel. The man serving you a beer at the ballpark. Think differently. Think about your Unitization of Money and be intentional about porting that numerator onto other people's denominators. Along these lines, I always have cash on me. But I only carry \$20s and \$100s. The outer bills are $20 bills; the inner ones are $100s. It makes my daily tipping super easy and impactful.

GOING CUSTOM

Have a mindset and a system when it comes to tipping. I've described mine in detail, but here are some highlights: Minimum tips depend on the meal. For someone who takes my bags at a hotel or a bartender, the minimum tips are, like, 5-10x what is "expected/normal." The real trick. And this is the beauty. Add up your expected cumulative total in a year. And then apply the 3 Digit Rule and Unitization of Money. It's amazing and gratifying. Go custom on the keypad every time. And be prepared with the denominations that are in your wallet, so it's easy to access the tip you already know you want to give out, on a moment's notice. It should become second nature. I estimate that I spend an extra $30,000 to $40,000/year on tips. But I believe I make 300 to 400 people's days, weeks and months better.

Before we close this section out, I want to be clear. This is NOT tipping for better service. This is meant to be all about taking that water droplet from your bathtub or glass, where it's indiscernible, and placing it in the teaspoon, where it is meaningful and visible. It's a Random Act of Daily Financial Kindness. Different.

But I'll riff for a second around tipping for a service exchange to demonstrate the trappings of putting certain numerators over different denominators. There's an amazing all-inclusive resort we've been to many times. Some call it the Four Seasons of all-inclusives. I'm not sure I'd go that far, but it's a great spot. But, like a lot of resorts, you have to deal with the dreaded "Who's gonna wake up at 6 a.m. and get us our lounge chairs by the pool" dynamic. So, on our second visit (we've been there a few more times since then), I applied some of my logic to the conundrum. It's all inclusive, so when the "bill" comes at the end of the day to your seats, it's a zero balance, of course. So, the first year we were there, waking up at the crack of dawn for our sub-optimal seats, I'd usually scribble $25 or maybe $50 each day. I don't really remember. But in our second year, I adopted a different philosophy. We were going to be there for six days. I think the total for both rooms that year was $37,000 for the week. So, I said to myself, "Why not pretend there is a $1,500 add-on package which guaranteed you exactly the seats you wanted, and you could sleep in to 10 a.m. And not only would you get those seats every day, but you'd also get amazing service by your seats, in the pool and even get some off-menu items for lunch!" My gut is if that were a box you could check during checkout, many people would opt for it. But, of course, it's not. This is fictitious. But perhaps if I scribbled $250 each day on the tip line of the $0 balance check, I'd get that exact "package." And I did. And it worked.

A few days later, another family saw me and said, "If you don't mind, how do you get these seats every day?" I sorta smiled and he said, "OH, you tip the guys. So do I." And I said, "If YOU don't mind, what do you tip every day?" He said, "Twenty bucks. How much do you tip?" I said, "More than 10x that." He looked at me like I was crazy, but then I broke it down the way I described above. And he looked at me and immediately said, "Holy shit! I'm an idiot."

He wasn't an idiot (well, he may have been, but I'm not judging based on this episode). He just fell into the trap of mental anchoring and looking at relative percentages derived by porting numerators on top of different denominators. For $38,500, I had a radically different experience than the $37,000 rack rate on the website!

CHAPTER 13

PATIENT 1,001

0[73] The Sahara

I remember the first time it happened. Well, not the actual first, like most recollections. It's funny how people start sentences that way but don't ACTUALLY remember THE first time. They usually remember more how they FELT about the first time, which is typically an amalgamation of all the superlative qualities of that thing they're discussing.

So, during that first time, I woke up with this pretty intense itchy pain. I'll spare you exactly where it was. I think I looked for some type of moisturizer as my 2 a.m. brain felt I was clearly lacking some moisture, so I might as well try to convert my desert situation into some other type of climate. So, I applied some, the itching finally dissipated, and I fell back asleep.

I woke up 4 hours later, likely by an alarm. Dana and I were getting ready for our day, and I told her about the episode. She was sorta concerned, sorta grossed out. She sorta thought it was funny, well, because we all still giggle about shit like this. So, I asked, "Umm, whom do you think I should call?" She immediately said,

"Dr. XX, she's the best dermatologist."

She probably called for me after I forgot to do it for days. I got to the doctor's office that week or the following one, checked in and waited. Then I was called into an office and asked to put on the robe. I always find this dynamic weird. You're there to talk about a hangnail that's infected. "Please put on your robe, sir, and just keep your underwear on."

You come in to talk about an ongoing headache and it's, "Sir, please take off all your clothes except your underwear and put on this gown." No matter what the ailment, it's always "Take off your clothing and awkwardly sit in the robe."

Also, how are you supposed to tie it, exactly? Opening in the back? Opening in the front? If the back, if you're inflexible like me, what do you do?

So, I was in a white room I'd never seen before, having sat in a waiting room I'd never been in before and checked in with a receptionist I'd never talked to before. In walked a person I'd never seen before. She was wearing a white coat. I quickly explained the Sahara Desert situation, and suddenly, I was showing this person I'd only met a minute or two earlier the rash. (Many, many years later, I had an epiphany about this episode, which helped me form two major frameworks related to why the hell my brain told me it was safe to literally expose myself in every way to this woman I didn't know and trust she was equipped to help me? But more on that later).

0^{74} A little empathy, Doc?

So, she quickly inspected my nether regions, and without much analysis, was like, "Oh, I see this all the time. No big deal. It's just an eczema patch. I have some good meds for that. Make sure not to use too much, or it can thin and possibly perforate the skin, but you should be fine. Nice meeting you. Have a great day."

And just like that, she was gone. It was interesting. I came to her because somehow, I thought she was an expert (we'll get to this in a bit), but she made me feel like a number. I, of course, wanted someone who had seen this ailment one hundred times. But I didn't like feeling like number one hundred and one.

YOUR ONE AND ONLY

Remember this is your one and only life (at least as far as we know). Don't let anyone ever make you feel like a number. Whether it's a doctor. A service provider. Things like that. It doesn't feel good. And remember this in your life, when YOU are the advice giver. Because of your success, you are likely sought out for advice and perhaps give some unsolicited, with good intentions. While pattern recognition is important, I always say: Everyone wants advice from someone who's seen 'it' 100x..but doesn't ever want to feel like number 101.

0[75] When it's the 1,001st time

Believe it or not, this episode shaped how I think about working with clients as a wealth advisor. Meaning, clients come to me because of my expertise. They know I've seen it a hundred times. That's why they are coming to talk to me.

But how do you delicately balance that you've seen it one hundred times, maybe 1,000 times, without making someone feel like number 1,001? I tell my team, "You want someone that's seen it 1,000x...but recognizes this is your one and only life. The one and only time you are selling a business. The one and only of so many things." I pride myself on never wanting a client to feel like I did in that dermatologist's office. She made me feel like a number. No malice. It was just her operating mode.

Her approach is pretty common, actually, but that doesn't make it better. I wish I had said so at the time. In some ways, I wanted to look at her and say, "Umm, doc, this is my one and only body. It's great you've seen it so many times but have some empathy for how it feels to me."

0[76] The white coat

I also found it curious that I was so comfortable quite literally dropping my pants in front of this woman I'd never met, in a room I'd never been in. I know, "Adam, this isn't so weird, she's a doctor, what's the mystery? Why are we talking about this?"

I suppose because I found it interesting that my brain told me that I was in a safe place. It was okay to expose my most vulnerable bodily regions to this stranger, and she wouldn't hurt me. Actually, I knew doing that was the only way she could help me.

So, early on in my career as a wealth advisor, I'd meet people coming to our office with their own financial ailments and really couldn't always get to what was causing the pain. I was not asking all the questions I needed to, and more importantly, they weren't sharing the full story. Without understanding the whole picture, I saw it would be impossible to diagnose the problem and come up with a plan of attack.

The analogy of a doctor's office visit became very relevant. In most industries where you're aiming to provide advice, you don't get the proverbial white coat. There is no white room inside some doctors' offices. It was just me, in a WeWork or an LPQ, or maybe my own office.

I didn't wear a white coat. I wore jeans. But I knew that I needed to get the person to feel comfy enough to, so to speak, drop their pants.

So, around that time, I began to ask much more probing questions, voiced through the lens of curiosity, just as the dermatologist may have asked. No shame in any question, because the spirit was to be as helpful as possible. And being armed to be helpful means you need to ask a lot of questions. Relevant and seasoned ones. Expert questions.

It makes a difference. You always know that moment. You are in a conversation where you're trying to be helpful, whether in your personal life or at work. Suddenly, you look around and you've instantly teleported. You're the advice giver in the white coat. The advice receiver is in the robe. And you're both in the safe white room. That's the moment real advice can be given and received. It requires vulnerability. Trust. Expertise. And it requires finding the "right" person to provide that expert advice that is wrapped in empathy but steeped in hundreds or thousands of data points. That tricky duo.

0^{77} Experts

So, what I purposely glossed over and is another learning from this episode: HOW I got to the dermatologist. I love my wife to death, but why did I think my she knew the best person to send me to? Meaning, in hindsight, how did she know that this dermatologist was any good?

I imagine Dana knew the dermatologist had been doing this job for at least 5-10 years, so she easily had the proverbial 10,000 hours. Zero chance Dana was thinking about it that way, but I presume she intuitively felt the doctor must have expertise.

In hindsight, I know she also liked the doctor personally. The doctor was a suburban mom in a neighboring town. Pretty. Well dressed. Kids of similar ages to our daughter. So that was part of why she referred me to her. Well, not part, A LOT of why she referred me to her was because she simply liked her.

Now, that doesn't mean the doctor wasn't also a GREAT dermatologist, but I am saying that the referral came from a place that probably wasn't so relevant to my ailment.

Also, how many other dermatologists do you think my wife had checked out in the area before settling on this expert? Two? At most? She had not done diligence on dozens of dermatologists, showed them ALL the same ailments and THEN determined that her gal pal was the BEST of them all at helping her with said ailments. This, of course, is totally normal and how most of us operate!

So, if you think about the lens of due diligence, data points, sample sizes, all that fun math, here I was, going to an expert, who was barely diligenced by my wife and mostly landed on them trading Bat Mitzvah fashion and planning ideas.

I'm just saying that it was eye-opening when I reflected on this episode that I simply trusted my wife to send me to someone who would take care of me. And it got me thinking a lot about false positives we deal with all day long. Perhaps even false deities.

So often, we ask someone we trust and respect for a referral to an expert. But we oddly ascribe incredible value to that person's referral, even though the reasons we like and respect them so much have NOTHING to do with their ability to diligence the expert. AND, we have no idea how THEY met the expert and how many others they met. Like my wife with the dermatologist.

0[78] Patient 0

The area I've become an expert in is venture-backed founders and venture capitalists. I love this niche. It's a world where I've spent tens of thousands of hours and have seen an endless stream of data points. I pride myself on the melding of crazy pattern recognition with my guiding principle of this being every "patient's" ONE AND ONLY when they walk through my proverbial door. About 99% of the time now, it's a Zoom box, but you get my point.

So, I'll toggle around in the time machine for a bit. At one point, I was pretty entrenched in the startup community. I met an estate planning attorney who was similarly embedded. She was curious why we weren't doing more together, etc.

There were a lot of reasons, including being on opposite coasts, and, if I fast forward, we've since done some stuff together, but that's not the point. I'm not going to focus on whether she's an amazing attorney or not. What I want to focus on is WHY so many founders use her.

It's all about what I will refer to as Patient 0. At some point, some founders in the ecosystem needed estate planning, in anticipation of the eventual sale of their business or IPO. I don't know how they made their way to this estate planning attorney, but I'd imagine they didn't interview 10 to 20 of them back then. They probably got a referral from someone they trusted.

Whether that person was equipped to make the referral is an interesting question, but I don't want to start connecting all the layers of referral motivation and decision trees to past decisions, as it would lead to an endless cycle.

So, let's pop back to what I'll refer to as the Original Gangsters of startup land. They picked this woman to do their planning. And I started to see an interesting phenomenon unfold. I'd meet amazing startup founders. Most of the time, they'd done zero estate planning. But sometimes they had done some work. More often than not, it was with this one estate planning attorney.

So, I'd ask, "How did you find her?" And 100% of the time (no exaggeration), it was directly from these Founder OGs or one derivative from them (i.e., another founder whom I know was backed or mentored by these OGs).

I thought this was interesting. And also, really weird and illogical. But I couldn't put my finger on why…until I did. For some reason, all these very smart folks ascribed all this trust to the referral from these OGs, but the trust was misplaced. Of course, there was no malice there. Zero. It was 100% well-intentioned when a newer and younger founder came to them to ask, "Who should I use for estate planning?" and the OGs pointed them to "their person."

But what I didn't get was this, something that happens all the time: What does being the OG founders, who are AMAZING entrepreneurs (likely amazing humans, leaders, mentors, innovators), have to do with their ability to do due diligence on estate planners and estate planning techniques? Zilch. BUT. For some reason, others falsely ascribed to them expertise in estate planning because they were looked up to and trusted in a completely unrelated space.

Really weird. There's not necessarily a fix per se.

It's something I think we all encounter in daily life. Again, what did my wife know about diligencing a dermatologist? Nada. But I obviously trusted her. Knew she'd want what was best for me, but that had no relevance to her ability to give me a good referral. In my mind, her love for me and being the Westfield OG wife made me trust the referral.

Now, in reality, I'm guessing we all make our way to reasonably good people all the time. Practically speaking, it would be impossible to seek out the right expert for each thing. But that doesn't mean we can't be aware of whom we are asking for referrals, how equipped they are to make a referral AND what might be motivating their referrals, as well.

By the way, when I started pushing some of these entrepreneurs on why they used that attorney, they'd start by saying "Well, XX used them." And I'd say, "And?" And they'd say, "Well, Adam, they're the best founders." And I'd say, "And?"

And there would be this funny, mildly awkward stare down until the irony was palpable and actualized. What the hell did their being amazing founders have to do with being trusted to make a referral to an attorney? Nothing. All this is meant to make you think, not necessarily to do things differently. Just be intentional and aware as you think about who you are asking for what.

FALSE DEITIES

Most of us need recommendations in some area of life. They could be for a doctor. A restaurant. A vacation spot. A service provider. Be mindful of whom you are asking and why. They may be a mentor. Someone you look up to. Someone you think is "ahead of you" on the journey.

While they may offer some good leads, this can get very tricky. Be careful not to overvalue their advice and recommendations. Think about their perspectives and superpowers that led you to seek their referral in the first place and ask, "Does that arm them to give me the most appropriate recommendation for me?" Often, people falsely ascribe expertise about just about everything on the planet to someone they admire. And remember, that person could be YOU.

0^{79} I've got a guy

We all know this person. It's a friend. A colleague. They have "a guy" for everything. They also know the best deals on plane tickets or credit cards. They know the most underpriced wine, etc. I think a lot about the episodes I describe above. My wife with her dermatologist. The Startup OGs with their estate planning attorney. What motivates people to make referrals?

In my wife's case, the reality was simple and pure. She believed the doc she found was the best. She wanted to help me. Simple. For the Startup OGs, my gut told me there is a lot of that. They care about the founders they are mentoring or perhaps investing in…and want to help them. They "believe" they have the right expert. AND they also likely enjoy a different motivation. They enjoy being "in the know" with the "right person." There's that other motivator of the consummate referrer of people and things.

So, I thought about this a while ago and still actively use this framework. What motivates people to refer, introduce, etc. While it's more complex, I'm sure, I came up with this basic spectrum of motivations:

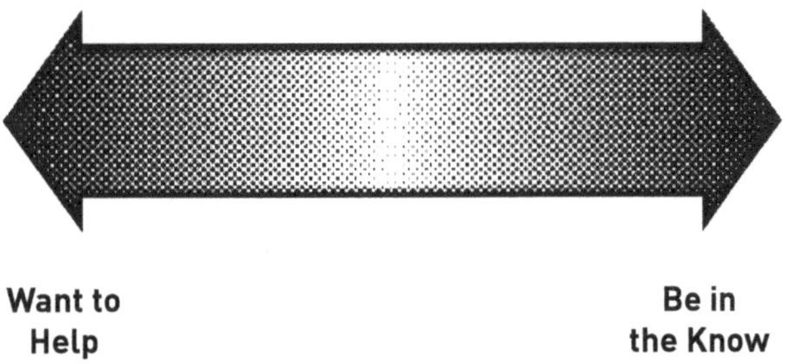

And I think it's as simple as that. Most of the time, when someone is making a referral, some dosage of "wanting to help" and "liking being in the know" is what's driving them. It's probably rare that either bookend is 100% of one or the other, but likely there is some combination. I think that's okay, and it's important to be active on this spectrum when asking for a referral or an introduction. Now let's focus on expertise: why it matters and when it matters most!

THE "BEING IN THE KNOW" SPECTRUM

When seeking any recommendation, remember that there is an easy-to-visualize spectrum that is likely motivating someone's ideas. The most extreme bookends are simple. The person who simply wants to be helpful. An individual who likes to be seen as the person in "the know" about everything, before everyone else has yet to discover it. Be mindful of this and think about what is likely motivating the person giving you the advice. Most people live somewhere on this spectrum, not the bookends. But pay attention when it seems that someone's motivations are likely heavily weighted on the "in the know" end.

0^{80} Friends are the WORST advice givers

As the saying goes, "Keep your friends close, your enemies closer." Not sure that will matter with this observation. But oddly, perhaps it will.

One thing I hear a lot is that "My friend told me about this." I conjure my good friend Ed, whom I talk about a few times in this book. He helped shape some important (well, at least important to me) elements of my mindset.

During what I'll just call the "management era" of my career (i.e., the first 12 years of working at Merrill Lynch, 1998-2010, ages 22-34), he once called me out on something super interesting. He had gotten a call from someone I had talked to that day. This person had, in turn, called him, all excited.

I don't recall what business she ran, but I must have had a convo with her that day and given some version of what I thought she should do with her business. Among those who have worked with me, or for me, or for whom I've worked (I still have some weird tic even saying those words "worked FOR," hence, the independent career path I eventually took) all would likely agree I have a fair amount to say. I'm very passionate about my ideas. I have strong conviction. And speak in an unusual manner. Both my tonality, my sentence structure, my word choice, my analogies (i.e., this whole book). They're unique. And my conviction-laden delivery is often mistaken for a stubborn, boulder-sized immovable opinion. I always explain that I tend to have a point of view. I've often spent a bunch of time thinking and digesting patterns of behaviors and information. And eventually I'm able to tie shit up into a very nice, crisp, satin bow. But man, if I learn new data points, I can change my mind quickly. I'm decisive, not impulsive.

So anyway, Ed got a call from a leader of some other business, explaining all the things she's going to change about it based on a conversation she had had with me earlier in the day. Changing her business because of ONE conversation she had with me. He listened to her for a while and then offered her a ton of counterpoints to things I had mentioned, taking what I'll affectionately refer to as "the other side" of the argument. And she hung up with him with her head back to where it started when she lifted it off the pillow that morning, before she had talked to me, full steam ahead once again with her original business plan.

He explained to me that my style of speaking was extremely persuasive. And that people often became enchanted with my words and direction. And that it was pretty dangerous, if not tempered.

At first, I didn't really get it. I felt that if someone didn't like what

I was saying, they didn't have to listen. They didn't have to buy into my ideas. They should have their own view.

But he reminded me, a lot of people don't. And if you are persuasive in your delivery and the words spoken, people will often take your lead. And it's important to always provide a balanced view of your opinions, expressing the counterpoints.

Which brings us to this next concept.

Think of yourself in a conversation with a friend. An acquaintance. Really, anyone who wants to hear what comes out of your resonant vocal cords. You're telling them about how they should think about vacationing. How to invest their 401(k). Something about their child-rearing strategy. Something substantive. Not what book to read or resort to go to. Something a bit deeper with consequences if they take your advice. This is where shit goes awry a lot. And I think I know why.

Imagine a conversation with your investment banker friend. And she's adamant about how the economy is going and things you should invest in and AVOID. You hang onto her every word, because you're a tech founder and you know shit about any of this. And you take her advice. Here are the two problems with that conversation:

Problem #1: She only gave you her points, not any of her COUNTERpoints. Meaning, if you asked her, "Hey, can you stand up, and pretend you are on a debate stage, and walk to the other side of the table and now tell me every reason to NOT listen to what you just told me," I bet she'd sound pretty convincing about the opposite takes on everything she just recommended. Friends don't give you the "con" list of everything they believe in and want to tell you about. They only focus on the "pro" list of the two columns. It's not done with any malice, but it's reality. So that's the first problem.

Problem #2: Accountability is lacking. Meaning, let's even say that she did explain all the reasons you shouldn't listen to her, but you still do. And you make some moves. You buy some stocks, you sell some other stocks, etc. You LISTENED to your friend the investment banker. But she didn't know. She probably had that same convo with a dozen people over a months' time on the sidelines of little league games, at a backyard barbecue, etc. She can't even remember all the convos and definitely has no clue who listened to her.

And here's the rub. Several months later, she gets new information that leads her to fully, unequivocally, CHANGE her mind. Now she's literally living on the other side of the debate table, battling against her former self. AND, she has no accountability to tell all 12 people that she talked to that she changed her mind.

Doesn't mean our friends aren't well intentioned, but they're rarely professionals in the advice they are giving. And if they are, they likely aren't giving you both sides. I mean, who would? We tell people about the things we believe in, not the counterpoints. Why would we? That's a weird social dynamic, but its absence creates unintended consequences for sure. I'd imagine many of you ARE the advice giver a lot of the time. Be careful about how you wield your unchecked power and influence.

THE DEBATE STAGE

Think about your daily conversations with friends. You joke. You reminisce. You commiserate. You share. But a weird dynamic rarely comes into play. When was the last time you told a friend about something you felt passionate about? Something you thought they should do or try out? And then, after fully telling them why they should do it, you said, "Okay, now let me give you some counterpoints as to why you shouldn't listen to anything I just said?" The answer: never. In our daily lives, it would be very rare for a friend to give another friend all the "cons" to the "pros" of whatever they just told them about. This doesn't point to any malice; it simply means it isn't necessarily a balanced perspective. Also, remember it's also as unlikely that if you changed your mind about a topic, you'd go back to all your friends, and explain you've changed your mind. So, listen to their, and provide your, advice in this spirit.

PART 10

ADULTING

CHAPTER 14

SINGLE, MARRIED, WITH KIDS

0[81] Responsible!

There are magical periods of life where you are old enough to do some grown-up shit, but still not really a grown-up with any real responsibilities. Depending on which lottery you did or did not win regarding country of birth, you get to 16, 18, 21, and things start changing.

The government uses these ages as lines of demarcation regarding things like driving a weapon, electing crazy people and altering your mind and body with booze and various, increasingly-legalized drugs.

It's a confusing phase of life. "Ummm, so mom, if I go to college 100 miles north, it'll cost you half, and I'll get to drink legally all of college. Sign me up!" says the HS senior at Canisius High School in Buffalo, NY, about going to school up in Toronto, Ontario, Canada.

Weird right. There is some arguably fictitious "line" that exists that completely determines things like how much of your paycheck goes to the government or state, how your healthcare works and, in this case, when you get to start doing keg stands. As a guy married to a Canadian, I couldn't help but add this as an example.

More recently, my family went on an Alaskan cruise that departed from Vancouver. Well, now you get into very confusing shit as Vancouver's drinking age is 19, ours in the US is 21, and in international waters it is eight. Well, not really eight, but you're in the middle of the sea, right? Confusing, and also fun, for my 18-year-old son.

0[82] Behind the wheel

Let's talk about driving. I love it when we have these arcane laws even within the SAME country that govern the readiness of a human to operate a moving weapon. An imaginary line arms our kids in the US with the automobile weapon two whole years apart. Two years on 16 is sorta crazy in terms of the development of the brain for judging what works in a video game versus reality.

In our Pacific Northwest, we literally have states that touch each other, such as Washington and Montana, where the driving age differs by two of these very formative years. Live in Montana, and you're behind that wheel at 15 with your permit. 15! I was making some really dumb decisions at 15. I mean, they don't give you your actual license till 16, but wow. That is VERY different from the neighbors just 50 miles to the left who live in Washington State who don't get their keys to backseat sex till 18.

Case in point: I grew up in New York. The burbs. Like the worst burbs. Also, let's dive into people's amazingly obnoxious, misconstrued pride regarding clarification of "I grew up in New York."

If you're talking to a fellow New Yorker, the inquisition begins. "Where?" The "city." "Oh, Manhattan." No, Riverdale. "Ohhh, all the way up north. And are you in the Bronx or Riverdale itself?" It's pretentious as hell.

I was a suburbanite. Depending on who asked, I'd just say New York. If they probed, I'd probably say the "burbs." Then, if you met someone from Westchester, the hierarchy began again. "Oh, where?" Then I'd have to explain "New City."

Confusing as a kid, I might add, as I grew up in New City, not to be confused with the much cooler New YORK City. Anyway, point is, I grew up in New City, which was a Hamlet (whatever that is) in Rockland County, which is across the Hudson, on the Jersey Side, north of NJ. Part of Rockland is Suffern.

I bring this up for all the *Sex and the City* fans. I still remember when Aidan mentions his house "upstate" and it's in Suffern? "Dude, that's the BURBS :-)," I proudly thought and subsequently defended for years. Funny things we find pride in.

Okay, so back to the weird ages for which we have lines of demarcation in life, as well as on some type of "map" that was created.

I remember vividly when I got my license. I'm pretty sure the driving age was 17 in New York. I so desperately wanted to BLAST my own music in that Chevy Eurosport with the pop-up moonroof. Wasn't a sunroof. Didn't open. Just "popped" up.

So, I opened the door to my mom's car. Back then, most cars had cloth seats (at least the ones we owned). AND my mom smoked. With the windows closed. I can't imagine how badly it smelled. I'd become immune, but I have to imagine it was pretty nasty.

I got in for the first time by myself. I was an idiot. I knew I was going to want to drive fast. Then I turned the tuning knob to find some radio station. Crazy how precise you'd need to be, as it wasn't electronic. You'd literally scroll the entire FM bandwidth and have to stop as the music came "into focus" and played clearly.

It was somewhat fortuitous and prescient, as a scene in a movie yet to come out in 1996 depicted something similar (albeit it was Tom Cruise, and he'd just thought he'd signed Kush based on the good-as-oak-handshake of Kush's dad) ....and George Michael's "Freedom" was playing.

0[83] Luck

I need to digress here into "luck." Remember how it used to feel when NOTHING was "on demand" and you'd "find" that song you loved so much was playing. I remember being six years old, going down to the family room, unwinding the long brown cord that attached this weird push-button cable "remote" to my TV, and pressing some button to get to channel 37. There it was, Luke Skywalker on my TV, learning how to use his lightsaber aboard the Millennium Falcon.

What luck!! That feeling is WAY lost with "on demand." I'll bet I wouldn't have picked "Freedom" to be playing if Sirius, Spotify or even an iPod had existed back then.

But the feeling of serendipity and luck and "B'shert" was strong in that era. I still think now, it's funny how if you happen to still use terrestrial radio or "flip the channels" on a cable box, you can still inevitably find a song or a movie you like midway through and somehow feel excited and lucky. Even though you could have easily played that song or movie on demand from pretty much anywhere other than your car or your couch.

Okay, so back to me, having sunk into the nicotine-soaked-seemingly-velour-bucket-seat of my mom's Chevy Eurosport with the pop-up moonroof. "Freedom" was playing, and it was time. Windows down, probably for anticipated wind to blow through my gel-crusted-Lego-man-like-hair and to also simultaneously address the Virginia Slims stench.

I drove probably three minutes away from my house down to Route 304. It was the closest thing to a highway we had. And the light turned green, and you'd think I was at an F1 race (albeit I find it very odd that their race isn't started with green lights but instead the series of red lights going away...can't we even keep shit like that consistent across our borders of geography and context? I mean, everyone knows green means go, red means stop. Odd).

So, the light turned green, and I floored it. Now, it wasn't like a Fast & Furious moment. Remember, this was a Chevy Eurosport whose speedometer only went up to 85 mph. Isn't that crazy? To think now so many cars have speedometers (and the horsepower) to go up to 200 mph. But not this beast: 85 mph was the top speed on the speedometer.

I was curious, as any half-formed-brained-17-year-old-male would be: How fast could this car go? Remember, it was my first time out by myself, and this was the first thing I was thinking about. Not "Mom, can I run an errand?" Not, "Mom, going to Mark's house to listen to some Journey music together," which I recognize was quite peculiar as I reflect, but something we'd do. I mean, that wasn't just me and Mark. Right?

So, moving on, the race between me and the speedometer was on. The best part of this was the steering-column-mounted shifter that existed back then. The main "gears" were P, R, N, 1, 2, D. So naturally, again, first time by myself, I thought of all the driving video games I'd been playing and the "stick shift" or manual setting I'd of course use to rev through the gears.

So naturally, way before "paddle shifters" were mounted in pretty much every car (again, who's driving their Honda Pilot like a race car with paddle shifters in 2026?), and I started driving my mom's Chevy Eurosport like a sports car. So, I was flooring it in "1." No RPMs to tell me if anything bad was going on I might add, but the sound and smell were not good.

I didn't stop. No fucking way. I "shifted" an unshiftable car by pulling on the plastic lever into the "2" position. Ahhh, the sound was gone. Phew. Same thing happened a few seconds later. Mind you, I was clearly not paying much attention to what was in front of me and what was in front of the road either. And I shifted again into "D" once the same sound/smell combo happened.

I was probably going 50 mph at this point, and it was literally plastic-pedal-to-the-nicotine-soaked-carpet. All the way down. Pinned. As hard as my 17-year-old-long-jumping-Achilles-calve-muscle could muster for my foot to stay on the ground. 60, 70, 85 mph!

Now, I was curious what would happen. And then it did. The seemingly 85 mph-pinned-needle of the speedometer started sorta bouncing off the bottom. Literally pulsating. Obviously, this didn't stop me either. Just wanted to see how fast I could go. Nah, I didn't crash or anything. Just slowed it down at a red light. All was fine, safe with my first experience with the rolling weapon. But man, I was quite the idiot. I got into seven accidents the first 12 months of driving. Most of which I never told my parents about and blamed on weird shit if they even noticed.

0[84] I met a girl

We all remember that part of life. Brain likely more developed. Mid 20s. And, you have a crew. Could be a crew of guys. Girls. Mixed. Doesn't matter. You are a crew. You have insta-plans every weekend. Your life pie is pretty simple. Almost 100% of the pie is you. Pretty selfish part of life. Makes perfect sense. Your folks are likely alive. Pretty healthy. You are just starting out in your "career." Main activities are work, sleep, exercise, and hang out with the Crew. Every weekend. What are we doing? Where are we going? Not "Do you want to hang out?" That's a given.

But eventually someone in the Crew says, in person, via text, whatever the medium, "I met a girl." A boy. A person. Doesn't matter. Point is, they have someone who's become a new piece in their life pie. And, by definition, other pieces need to shrink. It's annoying, but it's normal. So, that person is involved with the Crew's activities less than they used to be. Not 0%, but maybe 50-75%. It can creep to 75-100% if the girl/boy/whomever they're now dating comes with them. Pros/cons to this. And inevitably other folks in the Crew start dating people, and now you have a lot of different permutations. We've got OG Crew hangouts with the significant others. We've got coupling hang outs, which are Crew derivatives. Using my old high school crew, it would be me and Mark going out on a double date with our girlfriends. So, Mark and I are still hanging, AND we have girlfriends, too. Or maybe we bring them with us to a hang with our other friends. All is well at this point. Pretty manageable. Lots of similar hanging, not exactly the same, but it's still working. The folks in relationships are still relatable and mostly available to hang.

Jump to marriage. Still pretty good for the Crew. The married couples hang with the OG Crew a fair amount, and the married couples pair off with OG Crew members. But it inevitably happens. "We're having a baby," one of the OG Crew members proudly and frighteningly blurts out one day.

And now the OG Crew members have a problem. One life stage apart is manageable. The singles hang out with the couples. They can all go out till all hours. They can all go on vacations together. But now, the couple with the baby is constrained. That new entrant to their life pie, this bundle of joy, changes a lot.

It's very hard for the single members of the Crew to relate to the new parents. They can still hang with their married friends, but single-plus-married with kids gets tricky, given the flexibility and freedom of the single folks. It doesn't mean you can't bridge two life stages, but it's hard. It's not a bad thing; it's just reality. As we move through life stages, something similar can happen in your forties and fifties, when some of these kids start going off to college. If you are not intentional, this cycle can repeat itself with consequences that are likely more permanent.

0[85] Fridays

Fridays are an interesting workday. Pre-COVID, most people worked five days a week in their offices. If you live in the burbs of NYC, it required a painful John Candy / Steve Martin pilgrimage onto the magical island via land, sea, and through tunnels and bridges… and the occasional water ferry, after a drive through many tolls to find a spot to park somewhere else. NYC commutes are awful.

Pre-COVID, these commutes seemed to be necessary to access some career / job that was unattainable elsewhere. But at some point, you noticed some of your friends weren't commuting in on a Friday. That seemed nice. Ironic that back then, the idea of still commuting only four days felt like a massive win. And those lucky enough not to have to were targets for a fair amount of hierarchical envy. But what drove a lot of that, as people got into their later thirties and forties, is one simple attribute of their chosen career or rung in the ladder of the career trajectory: Flexibility. They don't teach you about this in undergrad or any fancy MBA program. But "time wealth" and "autonomy wealth" are real forms of wealth, as I mentioned earlier in the book. Especially at different ages and life stages.

So, it's Thursday night and you're out with friends, and you're packing it up at the bar. You start noticing some of your friends have less worry about getting up the next morning. Friday morning. Because they are "working from home." This is the first example that starts to creep up as it relates to what "flexibility" looks like at that stage of life. It starts to creep in when you chat about vacation time. "Holy shit, how much time do you get off?" It creeps into the sidelines of your six-year-old's soccer game. "How does he get so much time off to coach the team?" And that's on the Saturday morning games. Forget the stereotypical scene on a Wednesday at 3 p.m. when all the wives wonder "How come my husband is always working, and this guy is always on the sidelines in joggers. What does he do so that he gets to be here?" Crap like this.

But the point is, you begin to see that some people have arranged their lives to provide them with flexibility. Now, as life really moves forward, you can start to see this pop up in so many ways. It can center around kids. You can simply have an amazing family support system that is happy to watch your kids for date nights or even a vacation with just your spouse. You can see it with people having a nanny, which provides similar freedoms. And you can see it when people's kids go on to college, and interestingly, once that happens, they go back to the OG Crew. The single folks and the married-with-kids-but-now-empty-nesters are back to a similar flexibility, and perhaps are more relatable to each other than either is to the married-with-kids-still-dependent-on-them crew.

For this to happen, you have to stay connected for the 18-25 years in between (depending on how many kids you have), but it is definitely a full cycle. So, the point is, as life goes on, you'll start finding that some of your friends have flexibility mostly driven by their career choice, hierarchal roles in their careers and family dynamics (influenced not just by kids but also any aging/sick parents). To be specific, because we will get to this next, I am *not* yet implying any of his flexibility is financial. That dad on the sidelines may be a plumber who sets his own hours. That other dad may be a public school teacher who gets out at 2:06 p.m. every day. One dad may have sold a company and not have to work. It's important not to conflate flexibility with money and wealth. Yet.

When you have less flexibility than a friend/couple, you can still triangulate. You may not be able to coach the team, but on Saturday mornings, you're still hanging out on the sidelines. You may not get to sleep in till 8 a.m. on Friday, after a late night at the bar on a Thursday night, but you still can hang out. You may not be able to take a full week off to pop down to Miami, but you can fly there over the long weekend and meet your friends in the middle of their trip. Flexibility on its own is what I'd consider "life status" as life progresses. Not quite a "life stage" like single, married, or married with kids, but analogous and important to recognize.

0[86] Where are we staying...or sitting?

"This hotel looks sick." "These seats are amazing." As life goes on, another "life status" inevitably creeps in. Means. Money. Financial wealth. A friend hits you with a link to a hotel and you look at the nightly rate and you're like "Ummm, how about this place? It looks pretty awesome and is half the price." Or your favorite band is coming to town, and you get a ping about some amazing seats in the 100's section for $750/ticket, and you flip back to your friend, "Those $250/ticket spots are a section higher, and further away from the stage."

These little things start to creep into the Crew. The sender isn't trying to be insensitive. They just want what they want. The receiver isn't trying to be cheap. They're just focusing on what seems reasonable and within their means.

The disconnect can begin to widen quickly as life goes on, and financial wealth starts changing dramatically amongst crews. But having the financial means on their own isn't the actual line of divide. If you think about it, if someone has the financial means but no flexibility, there's only so much they can do with those means.

I'd offer that if you only have the financial means and no flexibility, you are still very relatable to your friends without flexibility and without means.

0[87] Life status

There's no form to fill, but I'd offer this framework for how to think about "Life Status" in your later thirties and forties. For simplicity, I'm using these categories as rough, crude groupings. "NO" doesn't mean zero. It means less. It means NOrmal:

No flexibility / No financial means
Lots of flexibility / No financial means
No flexibility / Lots of financial means
Lots of flexibility / Lots of financial means

Similar to the single person having trouble connecting and relating to the OG Crew member who just had a baby in his third year of marriage, it's hard for the "No / No" friend to relate and connect with the "Lots / Lots." Put simply, if you find yourself seemingly luckily in the "Lots / Lots" category, without tons of intention, your friends in the "No / No" category will likely find you unrelatable. You seemingly can be anywhere you want, doing anything you want. They have no flexibility to join you or means, even if they could join you, to do the things you are doing. This could be vacations. Experiences. Where you live. Etc. It's not a bad thing per se, but it is important to actively decide IF you want to bridge the gap of two life statuses (i.e., flexibility and means).

There are many ways to bridge these gaps, but it's hard. It was way easier to bridge the gap of one Life Status. The friend with the "Lots / Lots" can get an Airbnb for the friends with the "Lots / No."

Meaning those friends can get the time off, but can't afford the same vacation. So, the "Lots/Lots" friend can easily get an Airbnb and just say, "Get yourself there, and I've got the rest covered!"

LIFE STAGES/STATUSES

As you go through life, usually in your late thirties to early fifties, you'll find two things creep into life: flexibility and means. Most of you reading this book have both. You can be where you want when you want. And can afford to do it however you choose. The way you fly. Where you stay. Where you eat. But if a lot of your friends and family have neither of these things, you can become unrelatable. If they have one of the two, it's easier to relate on many topics. If not, you simply may be as far apart as a single friend and a couple who are married with a kid. Be mindful of this and understanding toward those you care about. You can help bridge some of the gaps here (paying for vacations, if they have the time off), but some of it will simply be the reality. Be intentional about discussing this with those you love and care about. While you can't necessarily bring everyone along for the ride, there are ways to eliminate the loneliness and isolation that could emerge.

0[88] The Scantron versus the blank slate

Isn't it weird how if I say "Fast," you'll likely say "Slow." Or if I say "Start," you'll probably say "Stop." Obviously, simple antonym word association is triggering these replies. I've given a lot of thought to the concept of mental anchoring in a lot of contexts that we've gone over. But there is one that goes on in our everyday life that is fascinating. It starts early on in school.

If you think about early parts of life, it's maybe elementary school when you really start getting "tests." They tend to be multiple choice, not "fill in the blank" or open-ended "essay form."

At the time, this seems normal. In fact, it never goes away. In high school, there are SATs/ACTs. Your written driving test. In law school, LSATs. If you become a broker, securities exams. Etc. Multiple-choice tests and options are everywhere in our lives, from our early formative years to some of the last moments as someone is picking out a casket for our lifeless body to rest. It's a fast journey from those early scantrons to the later ones. I think a lot about multiple choice anchoring versus blank slating via the empty, lonely line after a question mark on a test or in life.

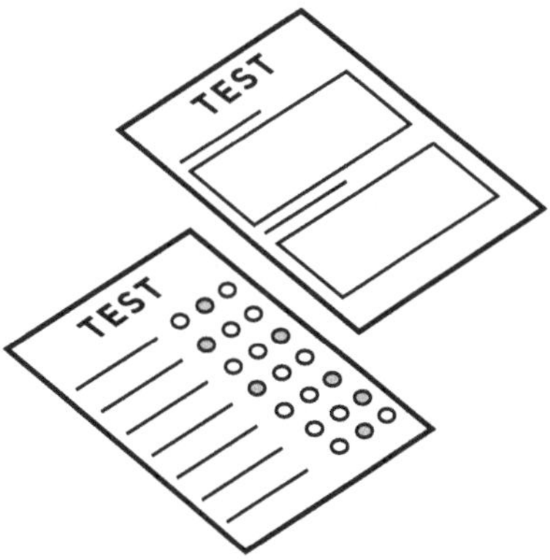

0[89] Who wants to go first?

Think about any group setting where you're getting to know each other, school, a job, a food tour, anywhere. The leader almost will usually trot out, "Can everyone go around the room and tell us something about themselves?"

Think about the ways this goes in a group of seven. Or four. Or 11. Doesn't really matter. I just picked seven, but let's presume it's a small enough group that you're not spending all day on this type of ice breaker.

That type of open-ended question is, by definition, a "blank slate question." As the inevitable pause button is pressed and no one speaks for a few seconds, eventually someone will either volunteer to go first or the facilitator/teacher will prompt "Who wants to go first?"

Now we all know the types that tend to "go first" in these scenarios. Kiss-ass types in school. Know-it-alls at work. Maybe just folks that have interesting ideas. Who knows.

Sadly, the go-first person tends to have a negative connotation. But what's interesting is that person is really the only one who is taking the "test" with a "blank slate" after that question mark. Meaning, as soon as that person gives an answer, most individuals in the group then simply anchor to their answer and give a derivative of it. These are not exactly limited, multiple- choice answers, but they'll now all likely be closely related replies.

In most cases, if that first person talks about their family, the rest of the people will, too. If that individual brings up what they do for a living, where they grew up, or their hobbies, most people will, too. It's an interesting dynamic, but also one that isn't surprising.

Most people like multiple choice tests, not "blank slate open-ended question formats." Once the first person goes with the initial fill in the blank, the rest now have the beginnings of a multiple-choice test. The last person to go 100% has a multiple-choice test, because even if #3 gets a bit creative and deviates a bit, that last person can't help but mentally anchor to the things they've heard and iterate and conform to what others do.

Again, try this out with some friends, colleagues. And watch this. How do you think you can make sure everyone goes first? Besides blurting out their answers at the same time? Go silent. Have everyone write things down on a piece of paper. And then have everyone go around the room. In that scenario, everyone has a blank slate. Then fill in the blank. And I guarantee, you will get a much wider variety of answers, even if a few people don't actually read what they wrote down and decide to ad lib.

This type of thing happens everywhere. Unknowingly, most people are going through their lives, taking multiple choice tests based on someone else's initial answers to the same questions, forgoing the chance to "go first" and "fill in the blank."

0^{90} SATs

Remember that time you were doing a math question on the SATs. As a reminder, I used to cuddle with practice Math SAT workbooks on my family room couch on the weekends as a kid.

But let's think about that time with some practice tests, and you see the problem. You start working out a math problem on paper and voila! The answer is 43,296! But then you look down and see these choices:

A. 56
B. 72
C. 29
D. 112
E. 2,096

UMMMMM...where is my perfectly calculated 43,296, Mr. SAT man?

After a few seconds of believing they must be wrong, you realize you massively misunderstood some version of PEMDAS, redo your work, and voila, 112 it is, and there you are, Mr. D. And your Number 2 pencil proudly fills in the bubble next to D.

Interesting. You 100% would have gotten this wrong with a blank slate, "fill in the blank" test, but because you had a multiple-choice set of answers to the exact same question, you somehow got it right. Hell, even if you couldn't figure it out, you had a 20% chance.

Now again, this example is not exactly where I'm going, but it is getting us into the mood. Meantime, how easy was it for people to cheat off other people's scantrons? It's like a pattern. You could look over someone's shoulder, to the side, all around you.

0^{91} BBQ talk

So, let's go back to the icebreakers. Not the gum. And not even the pathetic, contrived exercises forced upon us in new group settings. I mean life icebreakers. How about the most basic of daily interactions as you become a grown up. "Hi, how are things going?"

You might say that to a friend you bump into on the street or a relative at a barbeque. I don't know why I always use the barbecue as the example versus the cocktail party. I get that they're very different. And it's not like I grew up somewhere where a lot of barbecuing was happening. I just like it as an example. I suppose in many ways it's one of my many examples of trying to change the Scantron choices as a proud "fill in the blanker" myself.

Anyway, back to the inane "How are things?" question you inevitably ask and get asked throughout life. I often call people out as they get into their thirties, even forties, that they should probably stop answering that like they did in their twenties. Inevitably, a twenty-something can't help but focus their answer on something related to their job. It's weird. They didn't ask you about your job, but that's how you answered the fill in the blank. And so many people do this, so you can't help but think it's really a multiple-choice test that looks like this:

"Hey, how are things going?" And the answers must cluster around these choices:

A. Job
B. Job
C. Job
D. Job
E. Job

Now, I sorta give slack to people in their twenties, but if you're in your thirties and forties, and you still answer that amorphous, fill-in-the-blank test with an answer about your job, you need to step back and question your Life Pie allocation. Is there literally nothing else going on that would allow the scantron to at least have a few more choices, like these?

A. Job
B. Job
C. Hobby
D. Exercise
E. Family

None of this is meant to make people feel bad. Or like they are followers. These answers are comfy. Meaning, it's easy and comfortable to conform to basic sets of multiple-choice tests. We get conditioned to take them from a young age. But that mental anchoring towards predetermined answers or categories stymies creativity...and unnecessarily and prematurely makes people narrow and prescriptive on how they should think and answer questions. Again, I've been focusing on normal personal interactions, but in the classroom setting and eventual job stage, this happens every day.

0^{92} Blank slating

My team knows I love to "blank slate" people all the time. Rather than giving them choices, I want to see what they do with that lonely blank piece of paper. I'm not talking about the one with nothing written on those beautiful parallel lines.

Speaking of which, have I talked about my Parallel Lines poem? Remember we discussed my resume coming out of college and the two interests I listed there: Competitive arm wrestling and Composition of Mathematical Poetry?

I am guessing those words put together (not arm wrestling and poetry, I'm more focused on mathematical + poetry) feel like they came from a fill in the blank test, not a multiple choice. I don't think I saved the digital version anywhere, so all I have are some printouts. I used to tape them to my wall. In high school. That really helped me with the ladies when I was 16 or 17.

"Hi, wanna come over?"

"Sure, Adam."

"Hey, let's, um, hang out in my room."

"Adam, what are all those papers taped to your wall like awful wallpaper?"

"Oh, they're my math poems, how nice of you to notice."

That really got the ladies in the mood.

Anyway, I have always been a blank slate guy, so I guess it didn't seem so weird to me back then, and candidly, not so weird right now as I write it and fondly think back to those days. I'd been pretty prolific. Sorta like how I'm writing this book. I have always had some gift to think pretty quickly and to write very fast. Well not really write, as I can barely read my own handwriting at this point. But I mean type. Thank G-d I didn't cheat back in 7th grade typing class.

Wow is that an amazing example of how not cheating has saved me DAYS/WEEKS/MONTHS of time in terms of my speed of typing. I know, it's obsolete with dictation, but I still find it way easier to type than dictate. Especially on the creative side.

Similarly, for my Bar Mitzvah, I already knew how to read Hebrew. But when it was time to learn my Haftorah (the long "song" I read and where I sounded like Rocky), I didn't memorize it as a song. As most kids do. I'd imagine if you aren't Jewish, or are and did indeed memorize it as a song (likely with transliteration), you'd scratch your head here a bit and ask, "Umm, how else are you supposed to do it?"

Well, there are all these accents on the Hebrew letters which dictate the emphasis and tones you should use when singing the words to bring the melody. It's called trope. There are probably 15-25 melodies/tunes you need to know. So, as in my QWERTY keyboarding class in 7th grade, I chose to learn the trope tunes rather than memorize the multi-page reading as a song. I can still, 37 years post my Bar Mitzvah, pick up any Haftorah and sing the tune/melody by sight. Great example of not being lazy.

Anyway, back to the math poem era of my life. I often would write poems at night back then. No sports watching for me. I enjoyed writing poems. About math. So, the main one I recall was also most emblematic of the genre. It was called Parallel Lines. It went something like this:

Parallel lines

For what purpose did their originator intend their birth?
Was it a life of isolation?
Was the cruelty it possesses foreseen by its makers?
Sit down, Calvinists.
For what are you applauding?
A predetermined life of loneliness?
If only the lines were blessed with a transversal a slight bit less than right.

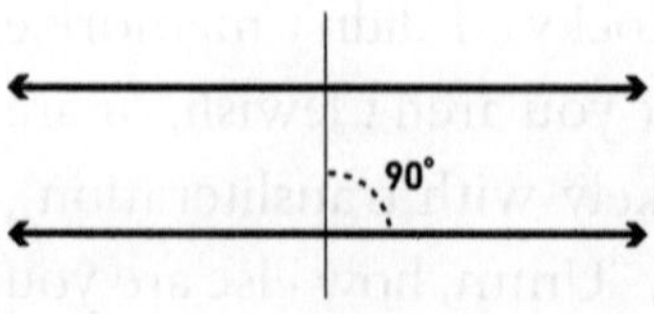

PARALLEL

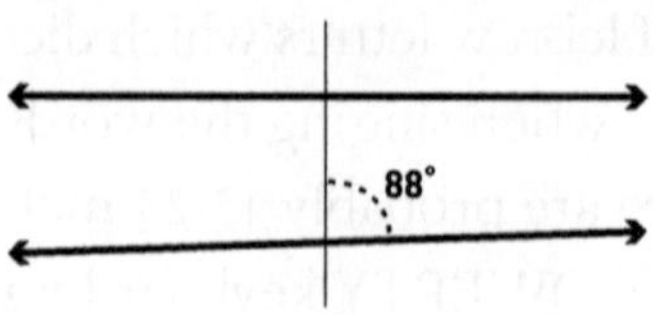

SKEWED

I don't remember the rest, but if the angle was under 90 degrees, they would no longer be parallel lines, but instead skewed lines. And eventually meet. I equated this to love.

Most people laugh when I explain this poem. Mostly the making-fun-of-me laugh. Also, probably the "Wow, my brain definitely doesn't think like that" type of laugh. I thought it was powerful. I imagine most of the laughter comes from folks used to looking for the scantronable life choices, versus the fill in the blanks. I never get offended. I still love this chapter of my life and clearly still like to talk about it.

So, my mom used to love my poems. Or at least pretended to. I'd run/walk to her while she was likely drinking some black iced coffee and watching a taped episode of Days of Our Lives. I'd settle in for the drink and the TV, and she'd read my poems. Nice memory. Formative in many ways.

Okay, so back to the blank slate concept versus the blank, lined paper. I love to "blank slate" people. This is never meant to be a punishment or a trick. It's meant to give someone a question. A set of facts. And get their own, original thoughts. Think about how often this *doesn't* happen in life. Most of the time, you're given some choices by the question asker. Or you're in one of those circles and you iterate off what other people said before you. I hate doing that. I believe it creates mental anchors and iterations of other people's ideas.

I'm not saying there isn't a time/place for that for efficiency or that it doesn't help someone make an important decision when something has already been "blank-slated" enough to cluster on common themes that then look like multiple choice tests. But I do think you can get the most expansive set of choices by starting a lot of people with blank slates.

Try it. You'll see the difference quickly. Try being the asker with a blank slate. Try being an answerer who will rip up the scantron. Walk over to the printer, open the paper tray and take out that glorious, 8"x11", blank, pristine, unadulterated, white piece of paper. And take out your crayon. Not the pen, not the pencil. But bring out that creative crayon and color outside the lines. Like a kid. Like I did with the Magnavator. Channel that part of your brain that lays dormant because of all the scantrons and multiple-choice tests that have buried them.

MULTIPLE CHOICE VERSUS THE BLANK SLATE LIFE

Don't get lulled into a life that's full of decisions based on what someone else did. I mean, that's okay for some things, but try to force yourself to bring out a blank piece of paper when trying to contemplate life decisions. In some cases, having some initial options to iterate from is helpful and time-efficient, but in many cases, it's very limiting. You can choose what you want, where you want, with whom you want. Don't limit your life decisions to what others have done. Be original. Be authentic.

0^{93} One-eyed Joe

We've all seen that scene in a movie. Where the bad guy dumbly hears the doorbell or knocks on the door. Usually, a door at a hotel or an apartment building. I guess sometimes a normal house, but the setting for these scenes tends to be high-rise oriented.

Ding dong. Ding dong. And the bad guy or girl closes one eye, and with the opened, exposed, super vulnerable, gross-to-look-at-surgeries-on that usually comes in four standard colors, sometimes conjunctivitis-encrusted eyeball, looks through the dreaded peephole. And splat. The other guy had their gun barrel placed about 2" away, through that metal door, ready to eject its eye-bursting, brain-shredding projectile through the easily penetrable glass peephole. If you think about it, it's nicely symmetrical. The peephole is by far the weakness of the somewhat otherwise impenetrable door. And the eyeball is really the main weakness of the otherwise pretty impenetrable skull. Anyway, this is a common maneuver in movies, one that we viewers always find peculiar.

0.94 The barista

I wanna dive into a quick tangent: the daily peephole that we all view one another's lives through. I'm not talking about the 12 seconds of a person's day via Insta. That one is obvious. I mean, that's not only a peephole, but also has a crazy filter from the best angle possible, etc. I'm talking about how little of the bookends of a person's day you see.

I think a lot about grabbing a coffee on the way to work, in my old commuting days. I'd walk up to the counter to pay and interact with a person who took my order first, and then the person taking my money. We would co-occupy physical space that is essentially a few feet away. It was 8 a.m.

Now imagine yourself there, close your eyes, and think about where you were an hour ago. The feel of the sheets you had just slept in. The water pressure of your shower. The warm car you walked into. The Uber that dropped you right outside the coffee shop. Now contrast that with the earlier hours of that barista. Think about where they likely woke up. What their sleeping conditions are like. How they got to the coffeeshop. The few seconds that you interacted were a peephole into the barista's life. Think about all of the externalities of their lives, especially where they pick their head up each morning, and put it down each night. The peephole is likely taking up 1-2% of your entire spectrum of vision into their life. Think about this in your daily interactions, and it will create a tremendous amount of thankfulness for your days' bookends and the grace you give others. Don't be an asshole.

0^{95} 50 to 60 degrees at most

So, back to One-Eyed Joe, which brings us to our elementary school protractor.

Yup. One of these bad boys. I'd say most people have a range of vision pretty similar to what you see in the full 180-degree spectrum of a standard protractor. Actually, it's a bit more, like 200-220 degrees with both eyes apparently.

But you get the main gist. Look up from the book now, stare straight ahead and you can not only see the objects in front of you, but to the side and even somehow, ever so slightly *behind* you. Pretty magical and something we all likely take for granted. But not in a selfish way, it's just how most of us are born and how we have seen for our entire lives. If you think about it, the friends who create our amazing movies and shows rob us of our full spectrum of vision. Forget IMAX. It's still irrelevant. Meaning, think about some of your favorite movies that made you scream or jump out of your seat. A scary movie. An action film sequence. Think about why it's so easy to get scared. Or get snuck up on. Because you're essentially viewing the world in a movie through a much narrower range of vision.

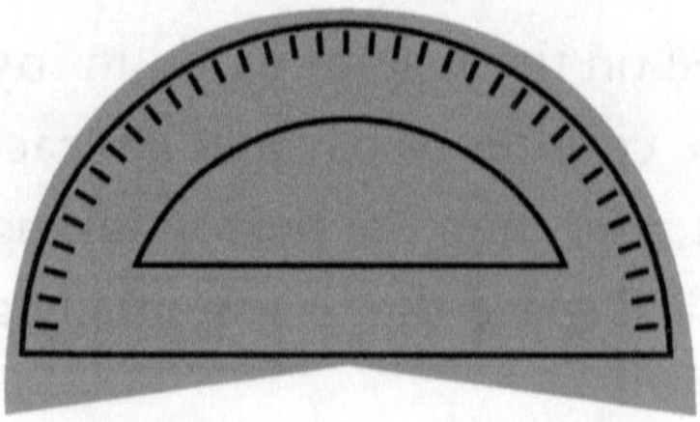

So, again, put the book down and put each hand up against your face, essentially blocking out your peripheral vision. That's essentially how you are seeing the world through the eyes of a character on screen. So, when they spin around and get snuck up on, or when something jumps out at them, in reality, it would be much harder to create the same impact if the movie screen allowed for the 200- to 220-degree vision. I estimate it's somewhere in the middle of the protractor.

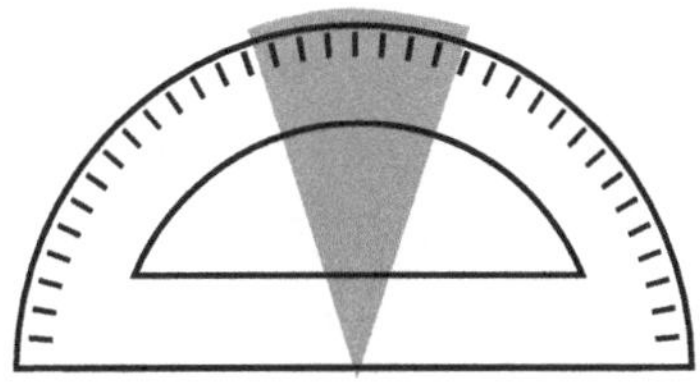

Probably the middle 80 to 100 degrees, 40 to 50 off the center.

Those lines depict your vision range in a movie, similar to putting your hands on both sides of your face, extending out so that your hands create "tunnel vision." Now, turn your head side to side with your hands like that, and you'll realize that it would be pretty easy for someone to sneak up on you. Or when you turn a corner, very easy for someone to hide in an area that should be in plain sight but isn't visible because of the artificially narrow band of vision we see things through in movies. Hopefully, that didn't just ruin movies for many of you. But check it out next time you're in the theater.

Speaking of which, I've, on average, seen 20-30 movies a year in a theater for probably 10-15 years (minus pandemic time). Mostly by myself. Mostly Friday afternoons. Wow, we're layering on this one, but I'm going down another path now for a bit. This one is super fun.

0[96] Unavailable

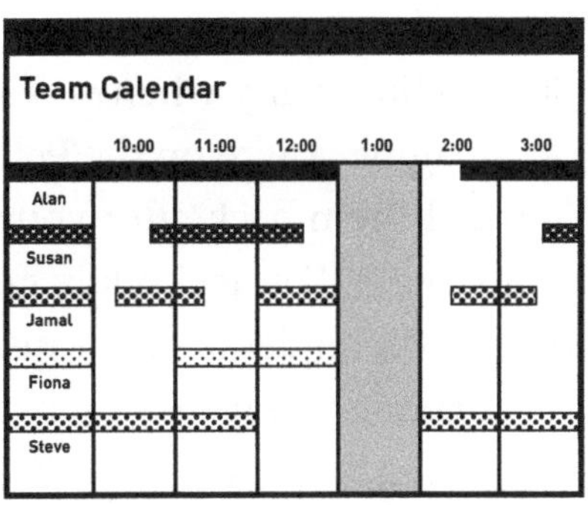

So, imagine you go into someone's calendar to set up a meeting with them. You see something like this:

Voila. We find a time that works for everyone. Looks like 1:30 p.m., it is! So, pretend you are the one setting up the meeting. And you find the time that works for everyone. You book it and move on. You give ZERO thought to what was blocking Jamal or Fiona between 12:00-1:00. You don't care because it doesn't impact you. Jamal or Fiona can both have other calls. Maybe a 12:00-12:30 and a 12:30-1:00. Maybe a 12:00-1:00. Maybe one of them blocked out a half hour for lunch. Maybe a doctor's appointment. Maybe a Peloton class. YOU don't care. And you simply don't know.

Now, I know, if you couldn't find time that works for everyone, you'd do your best to find one that works for a lot of you, then ask the person with the apparent block if they could move things. My point is related but more focused on the other side of this equation. Not the person setting up the meeting. Remember, they don't care what you are doing during those blocked times. They can't see what you are doing during that time. They just see you are unavailable.

And this is where things get strange. And I push my team on things like this a lot. For some reason, if we are doing something for ourselves – mental health, physical health, seeing a family member for lunch, maybe even seeing a movie on a Friday afternoon when things are quieting down – we feel guilty. But the weird thing is, no one cares. Now, I know, people are thinking, "But my customers or clients will care, Adam. I can't do all this stuff for myself during the workday!"

I'd challenge you to rethink that, a lot. For most people reading this book, you've had success. You have "autonomy wealth." Use it. Stop feeling guilty when you aren't available for a call on demand.

Imagine you're on the Peloton ride. A call comes in. You miss it. You call them back after your shower. Maybe it's 45-60 mins later. Who cares?! You feel oddly guilty because you couldn't speak with the person on demand because of the reason you weren't available.

Imagine you were simply in another meeting. And you similarly couldn't pick up the phone. And you called the person back the same 45 to 60 mins later. THEY don't care or even give it a second thought.

Whether you call them back after the shower post-Peloton or after a conference call, they simply knew you were busy. No harm, no foul. Obviously, there are some exceptions. Emergencies, etc. But this is a *critical* concept. Think about when you reach out to someone and they're unable to pick up. Or email you back an hour or two later. Or they look "blocked" on the calendar. You don't care.

Be intentional with your time and stop feeling guilty. To the "other side," it's indiscernible as to why *you* are not available for *them*. I can say this: Over the 15 years of movie watching, I can't *ever* recall needing to leave the movie for an emergency.

0[97] Blocking the calendar

It's important to carve out time for yourself every day / week. Don't feel guilty about it. It may be for a mental trainer (i.e., therapist). It may be to go to a kid's game. It may be to take an aging parent to lunch. Stuff like this. But. And here's the most important part. Just "block it" on your calendar. Don't feel guilty. Don't let it get moved. Pretend it's the most important meeting. You'd never move that if someone asked. Oddly, if we block the time out for ourselves, we feel guilty. Never feel that way. (A) you need these things and (B) the world doesn't really care very much. They simply see it's "blocked" and look for a different time to connect. That's it.

0^{98} Go wide before you go narrow

Bringing us back, heading up to the surface of my original point, we have one more stop. I can't unsee the peripheral vision depiction and not dive into another super important concept we've touched upon, but from a different angle. See what I did there 😊: The concept of going to an expert. Someone who's seen it 1000x. But not making you EVER feel like number 1,001. That one.

Pattern recognition essentially stems from having seen enough of something that in its raw form looks like chaos, but by seeing enough of it, you can wrangle some general themes or trends.

For my day job, I have insane pattern recognition given all the entrepreneurs I've met, at a very similar stage of both life and their business. Based on these experiences, I have a relatively good sense of things that will matter to them most and how best to help them. BUT. I always explain, before you get narrow and prescriptive, you must first go to the full periphery of opportunities, risks, etc. EACH TIME. Go wide. This is critical. You never want to miss something in the periphery, because you've falsely decided that part of the line of sight no longer matters.

So, to reiterate, getting narrow and prescriptive immediately is lazy and impersonal. Learn about people. Ask questions. Don't abandon your expertise. Don't look at things through the eyes of a movie viewer with tunnel vision.

Okay, one more before we get to the main theme. Can't help myself. It fits in too well.

You cannot connect the dots you cannot see

Holy shit! This is literally one of my most favorite frameworks. Some people don't like that it has a negative word in it – CANNOT. But I love it. And it hits home.

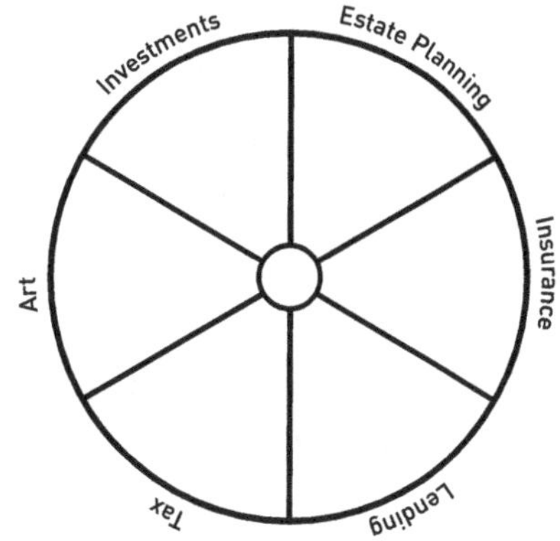

I came up with this about a decade or so ago. I drew something like this:

I explained that as a financial advisor, most people sit inside that teeny tiny circle. That's them. The rest of the circle is ALL the *stuff* a client needs. Also, all the *oth*er people the client likely needs in their life.

So, that's the normal Advisor, I said. That teeny tiny little circle in the middle. Now. MOST financial advisors you meet with tell you they are holistic. A lasting buzzword in the industry. They'll tell you they'll look at everything about your financial life. And will then say they help you with estate planning, asset protection, lending, etc., etc.

But what they really are is a human search engine. Now, that's not awful. At least most are mentioning all these concepts and needs. But then…and this is the crucial part that applies to my world, and I'd imagine many others. They simply refer you to someone. That's it. Done. They simply refer you to an estate planning attorney to help with a wealth transfer technique, and voila! They've "done" your estate planning. Again, better than nothing, but now I'm going to open your irises. Let's put all the players who help with each respective part of the client needs spectrum in those pie pieces to start making the point:

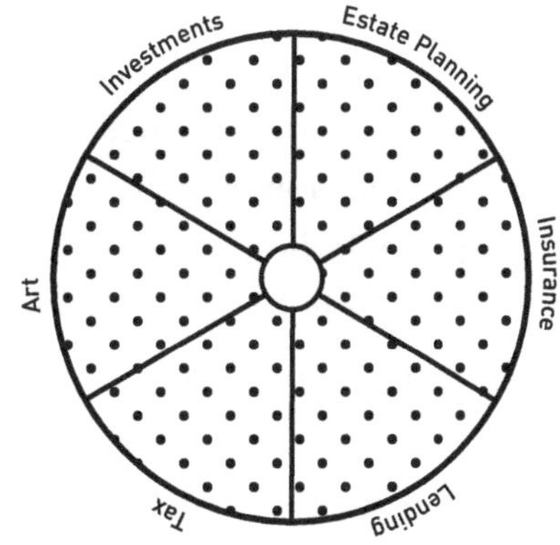

So, here's the problem in this scenario. Who's connecting the client's life dots? Meaning: Do you think the mortgage broker is talking to the trust and estate attorney about how the house should be owned? An LLC? Is it an irrevocable trust for the kids that the parents now need to "rent" from them. Do you think they're calling the property and casualty broker to make sure everything is now sitting properly under the umbrella policy? Nope. Never. Just doesn't happen. Each part of this pie, except for the teeny tiny financial advisor, is episodic and transactional. So. How can you change this?

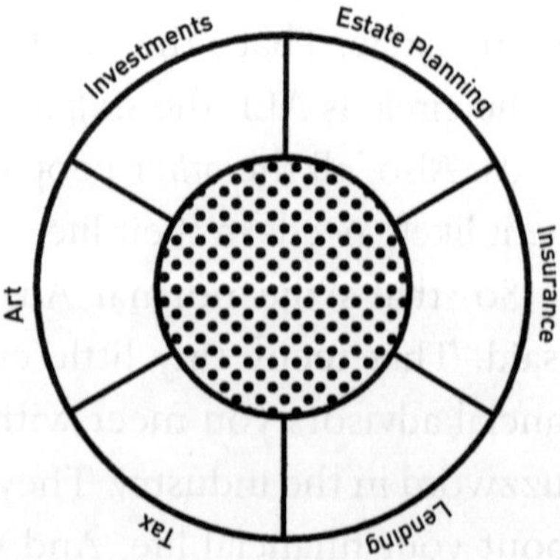

0[99] The ice cream cone

I was sitting with a buddy over some crappy sushi in a lame rendition of Stone Street vibe next to the relocated Goldman building. I had been getting to know him for the past year. Early in my journey as a wealth advisor. This was an easy spot to meet up for lunch. This episode was probably nearly 15 years ago. He is still a good friend to this day and now has five children.

But back then, he wasn't even married and asked me a question, since I already had two. Now, to set the stage, this guy was and is a winner. In every sense of the word. He went to a top 10 college. Was in one of their hardest schools. Was valedictorian. Smart. Analytical. So here was the question: "So Adam, I read a study that the 18 years of your child's lives are miserable for you and your spouse, and therefore I'm considering having no kids."

It wasn't exactly worded that way, but it was the gist. He wanted to know my opinion, having been an entrant at that point, ahead of him, in the parenting journey. My reply wasn't really what he (or I) expected to come out of my mouth, but a lot of my general ideas and frameworks are instinctual and get refined over time. But the rawest version went something like this.

"Jim. You are thinking about this all wrong. And let me explain. Right now, think about your highest highs and lowest lows. Now think about your eight-year-old self. Elation was getting an ice cream cone and sorrow was that same ice cream cone, slipping out of your hand, and flopping sadly to the pavement below, with the cone's only prior existence known by the almost candle-wax-like-ice-cream drippings still all over that very hand whose weakness led to the premature demise of treat you are now mourning, on the pavement, rather than in your belly. That's it. That's your bandwidth at eight years old. Elation to sorrow.

"Now Jim, you're 25 and I'm confident that the "Elation <> Sorrow" spectrum has widened from when you were eight. You experience higher highs and lower lows than your eight-year-old self could. But here's the rub. NONE OF THAT compares to the exponentially widened bandwidth of the "Elation <> Sorrow" spectrum once you have a child. What you feel for them massively trumps the emotions that you can feel for yourself. And that, my friend, is one of the many reasons having children is amazing."

He got it. It computed. And as I mentioned above, he's had five children since. I won't say this framework was the impetus for his above-average procreation rate, but I will say that this clicked. Of course, there is the widened "Sorrow" part of the spectrum that comes along with being a parent, but the joy and elation you can feel for your child massively trumps what you can feel for yourself.

Meantime, it's funny how this ice cream cone visual sticks in my brain and has been a main focal point for some numerator and denominator convos and the 3-digit rule. Who would know a benign ice cream cone would have so much affiliation with frameworks in my 30's and 40's around parenthood and marginal utility of dollar concepts?!

0^{100} Brady Bunch

So, getting back to my friend Jim and his questions about parenthood. Ironically, I'm sorta making fun of him up above using his Ivy League valedictorian engineering brain's lens to look at having children, but about 15 years later, I have an even more analytical framework of how I look at parenting.

Now, I don't want to conflate this with his pondering of whether he should even have had any children. I'm going to focus on something quite different. Before I dive in, though, I will get into a related topic, as hearing the word "parent" can't help but trigger my reaction to even hearing that word.

Both of my parents are dead. I wonder why people don't say it that way, by the way. "They've both passed." "I've lost them both." They're dead. As simple as that, but oddly that sounds callous.

Anyway, my mom died when I was 34, and my dad when I was 42. And I often say that I wasn't as sad about them dying as I think I should have been. Pretty weird thing to say, as you can imagine, even weirder to live. I'm not an emotionless robot. And again, I'm not at all saying I wasn't very sad at the time and still think about them often and am very sad about how much they have missed, specifically my mom.

But over the last year, I had an epiphany that has really helped inform how I look to occupy the role of being a dad. And that's just it; I don't want to just be a parent or dad. I want to be more. Mentor. Hero. Confidant. So many more roles. And that was just it, I loved my parents unconditionally, as they loved me. It doesn't mean they loved all my decisions in life, but they loved me. They were VERY amazing Jewish parents of their era. But...and this wasn't intentional, and I don't fault them at all. Zero...but they were "just" my parents. And because I didn't "need" a parent at 34 or 42, they didn't play a huge role in my day-to-day life. If either of them died when I 100% needed a parent (think <18-21 years old), their deaths would have hit me completely differently. So, I think a lot about how to occupy *way* more roles than just being a parent to my kids. And I also try to think about how to occupy way more roles than just husband or friend. Intentionality around this is a huge deal.

0^{101} Childbirth theory

So, now let's transition to actual parenting. The science experiment worked. Which I might add is also pretty interesting. Our physiology doesn't care about societal constructs or norms. Or careers. Our bodies are ready to make and have kids in our teens and early twenties. And those are the years no one wants kids, so we do everything we can to avoid having them, usually. And then of course, when "life" seems to catch up, having kids is way harder because our bodies and genetic code could care less about how much money we've saved, or the house we now live in. This is, of course, why there are so many fraternal twins versus when a lot of us grew up.

Okay, so we're at the hospital. It's time. A la Mike Tyson, everyone has a plan till they get punched in the face. I think a lot of people have plans for how childbirth will go. Their mind's eye has a whole narrative. Maybe you've gone to a bunch of classes, etc.

But reality is, you never know what's going to happen during birth. Breaches. Umbilical cords, etc. Fortunately, in most developed areas of the world, we can navigate this all skillfully. There's a mismatch to the emotions of the parents, but the actual science of everything is taken care of by the hospital staff. Why? Because they have done this hundreds to thousands of times before you walked in. You aren't a number, but you are. And here is the important lesson. WE. ALL. PRACTICE. ON. OUR. CHILDREN. Because in what other profession would having six data points, like the Brady Bunch (which is way more than the two kids most people have), allow you to serve as an expert? None. Zero. And here is where I want to dive in.

0^{102} The anti-soccer-parent

So, a client's son was going through some shit. Like a lot. And his parents fortunately were able to get him access to amazing professionals. Some heavy-duty PhDs. It was fortunate they could access them, and even more fortunate how well he reacted and adapted to a new lens to look at so many parts of life.

So, during one of the weekly check ins, the PhD therapist was saying something to the family and the dad brushed it aside. It was an outlier comment. Something like, "In my 10 years of doing this, I've never had a kid do what your son has done." To which the dad said something like, "Okay, that's great to hear, moving on." To which he pretty much said, "Neal, shut the fuck up and listen to me."

He didn't quite use those words, but that was the message the dad heard. The PhD went on to subtly remind the parents that he'd dealt with hundreds to thousands of kids like their son. Meaning he had a VALID SAMPLE SIZE.

Upon hearing this story, I had the epiphany that we all are FORCED to practice on our kids. But. And here it is. IF we choose to surround our kids with people who have valid sample sizes, AND …and this is the big AND…AND we empower them to be CANDID with us. Maybe, just maybe, we have a shot of getting a real mosaic on how our children are doing. Using your Financial Wealth to access these types of providers is critical.

This, of course, doesn't mean we take people's assessments of our kids as gospel. Listen, they are all humans. They have subjective lenses like anyone. I mean, less subjective than Grandma who tells you "They've never seen a smarter two-year old!" Or "He's the best baseball player on the team."

Of course, some of what the experts are saying is subjective. BUT they have enough data to give you a real objective perspective on how good your kid really is at the violin, or how good a soccer player they are or how proficient their writing really is. So, my main takeaway here, which has helped me tremendously in the "parent" occupation, is to surround my children with experts. Folks who have valid sample sizes. And empower them to be honest. That part is the hardest, not for me. But for them. Because most parents simply don't want to hear the truth. They want validation of their VERY subjective, uninformed, non-validated sample size of two to six-year-old versions of their child.

WE ALL PRACTICE ON OUR KIDS

I often ask, "In what other profession would having two or three data points make you an expert?" Yet with parenting, we are all practicing, by definition. It's extreme, but valid. So, surround yourself with experts who DO have hundreds if not thousands of data points. Teachers. Therapists. Coaches. And empower them to be candid about your kid. It doesn't mean they don't have their own biases. Or that they are good at communicating (i.e., your kid's soccer coach may not be so skilled at explaining things). But by being mindful of this dynamic, you can likely get a real picture of your kid(s).

0

THE FINAL CHAPTER (FOR NOW)

CHAPTER 15

SCARCITY VERSUS ABUNDANCE

0[103] Who's the scarce resource?

As I have worked on this book for the past couple of years, I realized that at some point, I'd need to put a bookend in place and call it "The End," like an old school silent movie's last frame.

There is no simple way to tie this book up, because it's not really "over." To that end, about six months ago, I started a "New Ideas" note on my iPad that will likely serve as additional frameworks for my own next chapter, along with perhaps a follow-up to this book.

But alas, while I don't really enjoy conforming to much, I realize we do need an ending of sorts for this book. I don't think it's artificial per se, but there has been a framework I've been noodling on for years and articulating out loud with vigor for the past three to six months that feels like a great way to close out the book. I'd say it's a pretty decently tied bow. Not from a Tiffany's box, but a reasonable six-year-old's new favorite sneakers type of shoelace bow.

As an aside, I'm curious how many people still use the two-bunny-ears shoelace technique versus the more four-in-hand style, almost like a tie. Speaking of which. Ties. Suits. Collared button-down shirts. Leather shoes. I wonder if anyone would dare to say they are comfortable? I know, I know. The materials can feel amazing. That's not what I'm asking. Who in their right mind would just pop out of bed on a Sunday morning and put on a suit and tie with uncomfy shoes? I get it that there's a mind-mode certain garb can serve, like its own time/space machine, transporting your brain into a different setting of sorts. But no one would answer that question with a resounding "Yes!"

This came up during a dinner last night with some friends. I was explaining that I quite literally don't own a suit. I'm a 49-year-old man who works in finance. I do have dozens of Hermes and Ferragamo ties from a past journey. They are rolled up in some bins and likely collecting dust, versus some splattered sauces at a lunch or dinner meeting. When I wore the silk chokers, I'd flip mine over my shoulder or tuck them into my shirt. Funny.

Okay, so back to dinner last night. My friend has dozens of blazers. I'm realizing I don't think I've ever seen him without one. He looks great. But we were talking about a holiday meal we were about to have with him and his family in a few weeks for Rosh Hashanah. I said something offhand like "Oh, I guess I'll wear my only blazer."

My friend looked at me with an incredulous and amused look, like "So, you don't have a Suit? What do you wear to synagogue? Weddings? Bar Mitzvahs? Funerals? Black tie?"

It was a fair question. I ended up explaining my "look," if you will. It usually would include some type of blazer (likely the only one I have), dark jeans, a self-proclaimed "cool" T-shirt with a graphic you could see with the open blazer (zero chance that button could hold back my current frame...not back to Sponge Bob shape, but definitely not quite the V-shape I was when I got this blazer tailored many years ago) and some sneaks. For some events, I'll wear a white button down. Never a tie. Not even a suit. And no shoes. Only sneakers. I literally don't own a pair of shoes. I probably have 30-40 pairs of sneakers that range $150-$1,500, with the vast majority closer to $1,000. I like sneakers.

When people ask me why I don't dress up, why I'm so casual, I have a few dumb go-tos. "My parents are dead, so no one can tell me what to wear." This is the first one I usually blurt out. I say it in a joking manner, but this is part of it. The other part is that I simply don't care. I'm comfortable. I'm comfortable *in* it. I like what I'm wearing. It doesn't feel like a costume or an imposter mask.

I'm not trying to prove a point. I'm not looking to disrespect the host of an event or even G-d. It feels authentically me.

But I think deep down, what's driven a lot of this is my comfort with not really *needing to* care what others think. Please note, this is somewhat different than simply saying that "I don't *care* what other people think." That is mostly true as well, but the nuance here is *not needing* to care. It has no positive or negative consequences. This is a somewhat nuanced take on a commonly uttered phrase of not caring about other's opinions oddly ties in well to this last summation framework better than the bunny-ears shoelace bow, after all.

What drives people's clothing choices, especially in a few contexts?

Business.

Milestones (i.e., weddings, bar/bat mitzvahs, funerals).

Vacations.

Probably a bunch more examples, but I'm too excited to get to what's next: the point.

I'd imagine that what drives people's choices are factors like:

- *Posturing* as to their success in life by wearing a fancier or designer version of what others are wearing
- *Expectation* of what the event's hosts would like to be worn
- *Blending in* with the crowd as to not stand out (i.e., a classic tuxedo and bowtie combo no one will remember because you look like you're wearing the required uniform)

There are more, but this is likely the bulk. And they don't all mesh together. The person who wants to make an impression versus the person who wants to blend in, are very different. But the various archetypes all usually exist in a given room.

I remember as a relatively young guy working in finance right out of college, I'd come home for the Jewish holidays at my family synagogue. I cared a lot about how I looked. Actually, let's be more specific. I cared a lot about how I *presented* to others. Remember, I grew up with essentially no money. Lower middle class. Never went on a plane with my family. No car until I bought my own at 25 years old. Public schools. School loans from college. I thought a luxury car was anything with a fold-down armrest. My hometown had mostly doctor/lawyer money at the top of the pyramid. No real wealth in the way I'd look at it today. I may be wrong about some outliers in that town back then, but in general, that was the demographic. But *presenting* as successful was oddly important to me in my mid-20s to early 30s. I was in a suit, shirt, tie, shoes, cuff links situation. So many wasted mental minutes to figure out the right combo. And the socks. How can I forget the socks? So many components. But the reality is the only two things I cared about were the ties and shoes. I figured it was hard to really know much about my suit, shirt or socks...but my Hermes tie and Ferragamo loafers were easy to pick out. I was so desperate to have those brands when I was younger that I'd buy the ugliest versions of any of them just so that I knew they were recognizable. And as I got a bit more money, I'd likely have spent disproportionately on those ties/shoes as well.

But let's get to the heart of why I was doing it. I felt like *I needed things* from others. Whether it was validation, a job opportunity, or a chance for someone to become a client, I was seeking my own version of a wristband I suppose. And how I dressed back then served as a signal. In hindsight, though, perhaps an unintended message, which is the heart of this chapter (and perhaps this whole book), is that I *needed* something. That something and the people who were gateways to it were aspirational. *They* were the scarce things. And I needed to present my desire to get access to their special thing, their scarce wristband, abundantly.

But along my journey, something happened many years ago. In some ways, it lay dormant in my internal self-mantras, but it was awakened a few years ago. This wasn't coincidental. It was when I sold my company.

By having my own step-function wealth creation event, I never really "needed" anyone ever again. I had a balance sheet that could sustain my lifestyle indefinitely, even if I wasn't working ever again. I didn't need validation. I didn't need someone to give me a job. I didn't need someone to become a client or a customer to generate revenue. It doesn't mean I wouldn't or didn't *want* any of these things, but wanting is very different than needing.

It was that point. That pivotal fulcrum moment when the seesaw flipped, just as it did when you were a kid on a playground.

That is the moment I want to close with.

Most people reading this book have built something. A company. A unique skill or knowledge base. A unique set of relationships. You were able to monetize them to create financial wealth that catapulted you into a new number of zeros in your bank account, likely suddenly. To build what you did, you probably were extremely abundant and present in specific parts of your life. With your current customers or clients. Your hopeful future customers or clients. Your team members. Your company. Your product. The golf course. Fundraisers.

But you were scarce "at home" along the way. To your friends. To your family. To your mental health. To your physical health. This isn't a criticism, it's simply a likely fact. Your life pie only has so

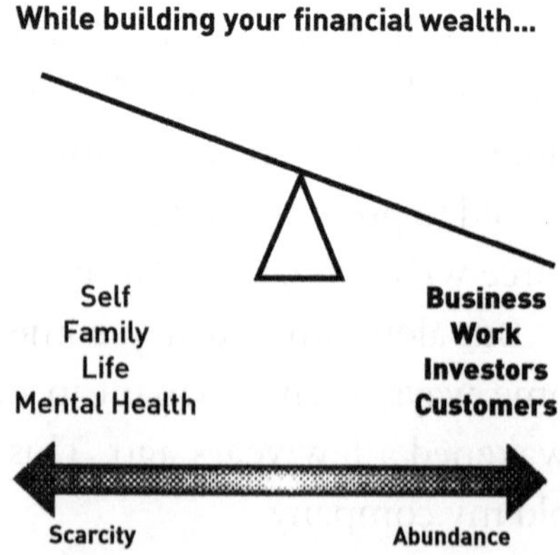

many hours and so many days.

BUT. And is the big ass but. The seesaw has flipped.

You are now the scarce resource. You don't *need* to care about anyone or anything in particular. Don't conflate that with my suggesting you go live on an island yourself. I'm simply meaning YOU are the scarce resource now. People likely want your validation. Want your business. Want your partnership. And some will also masquerade at wanting your friendship.

So, my last summation comment. Since you are the scarce resource, be intentional about your life pie. Shrink many of those unnecessary pieces. Enlarge and reintroduce the others that had gotten scaled back or discarded. Time with family. Time with friends. Time with yourself.

Time Wealth. Autonomy Wealth. Health Wealth.

Become abundant to those people and things you love and become scarce to everything else. You have earned it. You have the wristband.

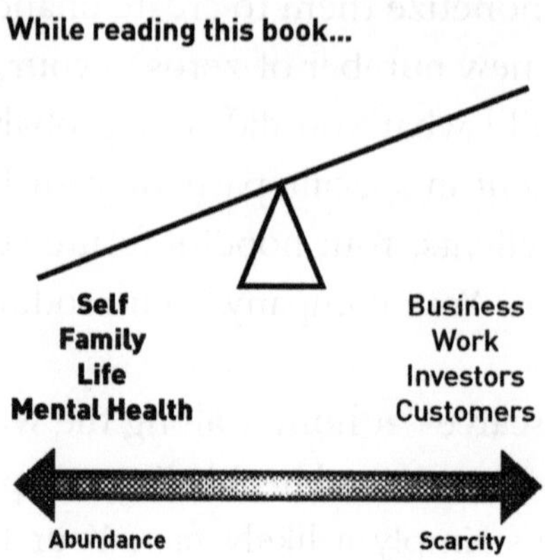

TIPPING THE SCARCITY SEESAW

There will come a time when you are the thing that is scarce. Not an elusive new client or customer. Not the next greatest product or service. Not some massive real estate deal. Not that hard-to-land investor on your cap table. It's now the opposite. You are scarce. But the trick is to be intentionally abundant everywhere you want to be. A hobby. With friends. Aging parents. Your kid's 4 p.m. soccer game on a Tuesday. Be there. Be present. Be abundant. And keep your phone on Do Not Disturb to most of the world, indefinitely.

INDEX

Mindset

Money

Careers

Advice

About the Author

Adam Katz has been married to his wife Dana since 2001. They met in Club Med in Turks and Caicos on vacation with friends — and the rest is not only history, but it also directly and indirectly fueled a bunch of what's in this book. Along the way, they had two amazing kids, who are now 20 and 16. Adam's own career, entrepreneurship and parenting journey helped shape many elements of this book.

Adam spent the first 20 years of his professional life at Merrill Lynch, with two distinct careers. The first dozen years spanned a variety of leadership roles within investment product, sales and strategy. He spent the last eight years as a Private Wealth Advisor. He and his team left Merrill in 2018 to form their own independent wealth management firm called KORE Private Wealth, which they sold in just four years in 2022, to what is now CORIENT. Adam is currently a Partner and Head of the Entrepreneur and Founder Practice at CORIENT, one of largest and fastest growing wealth management firms in the world.

Fun fact: Adam was the 2009 176-lb. New York State Armwrestling Champion (Amateur Division)

